North Carolina
Ghosts & Legends

Other University of South Carolina Press Books

by Nancy Roberts

South Carolina Ghosts
From the Coast to the Mountains

The Haunted South
Where Ghosts Still Roam

Ghosts of the Carolinas

**Ghosts of the Southern Mountains
and Appalachia**

The Gold Seekers
*Gold, Ghosts and Legends
from Carolina to California*

Civil War Ghosts Stories & Legends

North Carolina

Ghosts &
Legends

Nancy
Roberts

University of South Carolina Press

Published in Columbia, South Carolina, by the
University of South Carolina Press

Revised and enlarged edition

First Published by McNally and Loftin
Charlotte, North Carolina, 1959

Manufactured in the United States of America

05 04 03 02 01   12 11 10 9 8

The Library of Congress has cataloged the cloth edition as follows:

Roberts, Nancy, 1924–

     p. cm.
    Rev. ed. of: An illustrated guide to ghosts & mysterious occurrences in the
Old North State, 1967
    ISBN 0-87249-764-X (alk. paper)
    1. Ghosts—North Carolina I. Roberts, Nancy, 1924– An illustrated guide
to ghosts & mysterious occurrences in the Old North State. 1967. II. Title
III. North Carolina ghosts and legends.
BF1472.U6R636   1991
133.1'09756—dc20   91-14469

Photographs by Bruce Roberts

ISBN 0-87249-765-8 (pbk.)

Contents

Preface

Civilizations come and go but some things never change. In the midst of life there have always been and always will be ghosts.

There are also people who are more bold, more imaginative, or just more colorful than the rest of us. They become legendary and I find their exploits irresistible.

This book was originally published as *An Illustrated Guide to Ghosts & Mysterious Occurrences in the Old North State*. Since then I have gone on to write ten other collections of ghost stories and could not resist including a number of gold era ghost stories in my latest book, *The Gold Seekers*.

Several new coastal tales have been written for this revised edition of North Carolina's most famous classic stories, and the title has been changed to *North Carolina Ghosts & Legends*.

In addition to stories from the mountains, Piedmont, and eastern Carolina, there is a total of six stories from the Outer Banks—a unique and haunting part of the state. Among these is the intriguing tale of the ghost on Blackbeard's last voyage, a story with a contemporary historical source.

My first book came about as a result of personal encouragement from writer Carl Sandburg. It will always be one of my favorites. I hope that you will enjoy this collection of North Caroliniana.

Nancy Roberts

North Carolina
Ghosts & Legends

The Ghost
Comes for Blackbeard

Death and the Devil had done for the rest
Yo, ho, ho and a bottle of rum

Blackbeard had always liked the color of night, and it suited him well. He made it his habit to wear black from the crown of his rakish, broad-brimmed felt hat and thigh-length coat to the dark, sooty hue of his immense boots.

It was Friday, November 22, 1718, and he had no reason to believe that today would be unlike any other. The rising sun limned the outermost rim of the dark winter sea with a flaming scarlet border, and the ropes and rail of *The Adventure* glistened with silvery hoarfrost. Blackbeard's strong rough hands, thickly mantled with black hairs, traveled expertly over the rigging. From habit, the big fingers, half-numbed, checked the rope-yarns of the furled sails, so that whenever he wished he could haul home the sheets without his men scrambling up to loose them.

It was an old precaution of his. The lowered main and foreyards gave *The Adventure* the deceptive appearance of having lain at anchor for a long time. This morning, in the bleak gray light before sunup, he was a caged black panther pacing the deck of *The Adventure*. A tall man, he had a yard-long cutlass that swung on the belt at his hip as he strode back and forth with immense suppressed energy. The wide, wicked blade hanging from his belt had the slight curve of a saber but was actually a much heavier weapon, its rounded brass guard designed to protect his hand and wrist.

Blackbeard had taught his crew how to use these blades with brute strength and deadly accuracy. Sailors on merchant ships often panicked at the sight of the pirates' cutlasses swinging in murderous arcs, blades glittering in the sunlight, and many surrendered even before their ships were boarded.

The captain of *The Adventure* saw a pale, sickly sun, barely visible through the clouds on the horizon, and bellowed. "Israel! Israel Hands! Where in hell are you?" It was Israel, and sometimes the loyal, massively built Black Caesar, who often helped keep the crew in line. When the men didn't see action for a while, they grew slack and impudent.

Damn! Where was that rascal, Israel? Blackbeard threw back his head and took a great swig of rum from the leather flask at his waist, savoring the familiar fiery feel of it the length of his throat. Israel should be here to drink with him—keep him abreast of whatever crazy rumors crewmen were always whispering, or fight if need be, but the latter was unlikely. There could scarcely be a safer place than Ocracoke for mooring *The Adventure*.

And it ought to be so. He paid North Carolina's Governor Eden, who lived but a few miles away, well for it. Barrels of sugar and rum as well as other plunder were transported furtively by darkness from his ship to the governor's back door.

The heavy, dark rum had left a pleasant, lingering warmth upon Blackbeard's tongue, and despite a slight clouding of memory, he suddenly recalled why Israel wasn't there. When the weather was raw and the wind's icy breath blew wickedly across the water, Israel often remained in Bath Town because of his bad knee.

Long ago, during a gambling game in his cabin, Blackbeard had playfully turned off the oil lamp, shoved a pair of crossed pistols under the table, and pulled the triggers. One pistol misfired and the slug from the other tore through Israel's knee, crippling him for life.

"Why did you do that, sir?" a crew member asked timidly.

"So you'll remember who I am," roared Blackbeard, laughing raucously and slapping his thigh. Crew members within earshot melted away, stealing off to their quarters.

This morning Captain Edward Teach, or Blackbeard, as he was often called, wondered himself why he'd shot off the two pistols. Drink and the Devil, probably. Some even called *him* the Devil! Maybe they were right, he thought grimly, but a little fear was good for the crew—kept 'em in line.

Israel Hands had been a damn good fighting man, and despite his bad leg he could still swing a wicked cutlass. Why hadn't the shot hit one of the ruffians gathered around him instead? Some of 'em were better deck hands than fighting men. They'd have been garotted long ago, if he had not trained them well. Nobody would ever take *him* alive. He would fight until his last breath.

But today he couldn't get the superstitious talk of the crew out of his mind. It was on that last voyage from Bermuda back to Ocracoke that it started as a whisper. "There's one man too many aboard, a man no one knows."

Israel had told him what they were saying. "Well, blast them!" he had replied. "Let's find the rascal who started it, and I'll hang him from a yardarm. Assemble the crew!" Israel got together seventeen men.

"This extra crewman you think you've seen, men—tell me what the rogue looks like?" Blackbeard boomed out. But they stared off in the distance or down at the deck and none would say. Some began to slink off until finally only Israel and a handful of the crew remained. After questioning them and receiving blank looks or shakes of the head, he dismissed them, leaned against the rail, and spat into the water. "Yellow-bellied riffraff!" he pronounced with loathing.

His best officers and fighting men had left him, drifted off to join pirates of the high seas who had not accepted a pardon. Men like those would have told him the truth. Well, it didn't matter. In a few months, everyone would have forgotten this superstitious bilge about a mystery crewman.

He fingered the covered handle of his cutlass, its broad blade razor-sharp, and he recalled bitterly how he and his crew had agreed to the Royal Proclamation offering a pardon to pirates. Now he wondered why he had agreed to such foolishness. He knew it was the source of his restlessness and frustration, an act that would doom him to years of boredom—even to a wench! He grimaced. How could he have been fool enough to marry a fifteenth wife? Was he flattered that Governor Eden himself had offered to perform the ceremony? Or had he coveted the land that came with the girl, the sixteen-year-old daughter of a Bath County planter? No amount of land was equal to what he possessed when he stared out like this at the vastness of the sea.

He had found the people in the small coastal village of Bath both foolish and contradictory. They wanted to hang pirates if they caught them at sea, but when they met them ashore, face to face on the street, they thought them glamorous. Blackbeard soon began to see that he was treated as the town hero. He never ceased to be amazed at how the silly asses fawned upon him and asked nonsensical questions.

"I say, what was it like to be a pirate, Captain Teach?" The men would probe curiously, and women would look at him, asking coyly, "Do pirates really make people walk the plank?" He would reply with a chuckle, "Not pretty women like you." But now he was bored by it all.

He had chosen Bath Town as ideal for his purposes. It was situated on a river where boats could go up and down for pleasure but it was not navigable by large ships that might prove a threat to him.

Today *The Adventure* was anchored in Blackbeard's favorite spot—at the southern tip of Ocracoke Island on the sound side—"Teach's Hole," some called it. His elbows rested on the mahogany rail of his ship. He lifted his spy glass and pressed it beneath his fierce-looking brow, his hard, bright-black eyes searching the purple rim of the horizon.

Gawd! How he wished a sail would hove into view out there, and he could shout to his helmsman, "Chase the sail!" His crew would begin yelling, "A sail! A sail! Where?"

And then the excitement of the pursuit . . . giving the fleeing vessel a broadside from his ship's guns, pouring shot into her until the other vessel slackened her fire, watching for the right moment to throw the grappling hooks over the rail and board her by force. He loved to hear the earsplitting revolver shots, smell the smoke, and be in the thick of the screams and curses. His blood began to race just thinking about it.

He hungered for the feel of the hammerlike jolts to his right arm, the jolts that accompanied each cutlass blow as his blade struck or was struck by that of an adversary. Always he found his emotions surging to a fever pitch of excitement and intense rage that afterward left him pleasantly exhausted, temporarily surfeited with excitement—and substantially richer. Blackbeard's crew would share the plunder—gold dust, money, jewels, plate, wine, slaves, or other material goods. Without the reward, who would sail with him?

It had not taken Captain Teach long to find that he was not suited to being either a planter or a merchant. Pirating was what he knew, and he knew it supremely well. The blood of generations of rogues must flow through my veins, he thought, chuckling to himself, but so be it.

A few weeks ago he and his comrades, men who commanded the finest pirate ships along the Atlantic coast, had gathered at Ocracoke. Vane was there, Bob Deal, Jack Rackham, and scores of their crew members. What a party!

The celebration had lasted for over a week, and he had been host. Local fishermen who knew Blackbeard had put in at the island bringing fresh fish to sell. The crews of the pirate ships had barbecued pigs and cows. They knew they had nothing to fear with Blackbeard's own vessel, *The Adventure*, anchored amid their ships and the friendliness of the governor. Afterward the captains and their crews had gone their separate, predatory ways.

Today he didn't care if he never saw the town of Bath again. Here on the dark, gray-blue waters of Ocracoke Inlet he was at home. His entire being was part of the environment of the sea. His long strides adjusted to the familiar motion of his ship, the rhythmic waves surging through him matching the tempo of his own blood, the creak of the ropes—for years these had been a background for his thoughts. He felt intensely alive when he was on his ship. He lifted the spy glass again and stared out to sea—the habit of a lifetime.

He had thought of posting a sentry on a sand dune last night—the mast of his own sloop could be seen out at sea—but he had decided it didn't matter. He had been at anchor here in the harbor for six months. Why would anyone consider a pardoned pirate like himself worth the taking? Especially one who was received by the governor and the best families in Bath Town. His forays had been far and only minor—unarmed ships like fruit, ripe for the picking, that he had encountered on his recent trip back to Ocracoke from Bermuda.

He didn't have a full crew today, but the decks of *The Adventure* would be crawling with men when they heard of his new scheme. That would be all that would be needed to bring this ship back to life. Pardon be damned!

Suddenly a gigantic shadow fell across the deck, and Blackbeard's whole body tensed. He whirled to see a huge black hulk, a dark misshapen head from which stared two fearsome, glaring eyes, eyes that shot forth sparks. Long outstretched arms seemed to beckon. The eyes burned into his own and a thought seared his brain. Then the creature was gone.

On his last voyage had there really been an extra crewman aboard—a dark and sinister creature who only masqueraded as a human being when it pleased him to do so. Could it be that the Devil *had* come for him? Well, he would give him a fight—one that even the Devil himself would remember, for he, Blackbeard, was as intrepid as he was unscrupulous. From his youth he had possessed dash and courage.

He turned to see the head of one of his favorite crewmen emerge from below deck—the massive, courageous Negro the rest of the crew called Black Caesar. Blackbeard had taken him on in the Caribbean and he was one of the pirate's most loyal men.

"Caesar, you ain't afraid 'a that extra crew member the men have been talkin' about, are you?"

"No sir. If I see him first, he ain't gonna be extra. He gonna be gone!" Caesar smiled, and his hand grasped the handle of his cutlass.

"That rubbish started while we was cruisin' from Bermuda back to Ocracoke," Blackbeard mused. Caesar looked out to sea "Yeah, the crew began to whisper. 'There's an extra man aboard, one the Captain didn't hire on,' an' they was scared witless."

The two men lapsed into silence watching a puny sun struggle to rise. The captain thought of his forays the length of the Atlantic coast. Grasping his coarse beard, he rubbed it between his fingers in frustration. He couldn't remember when he had not thrilled to the chase, to the raising of the black flag, to the commands to keep firing until the other ship was crippled and then the order to throw the grappling iron over the side of a brigantine so his crew could climb swiftly aboard her.

Blackbeard thrived on excitement—the smell of gun smoke, the shouts and screams of battle, and the harsh metallic clatter of blades in fierce hand-to-hand fighting. He knew that his infernal appearance—the wreath of tiny flames that encircled his face from the lighted splinters of wood stuck in the tips of the braids of his immense black beard and the coils of smoke surrounding his head—was a terrifying spectacle to his enemies. From the first days of his career he had been a master at melodrama.

When a vessel surrendered, a rowdy, exultant cheer burst from *The Adventure*'s crew as their victims' white flag was hoisted. Blackbeard quickly inspected the passengers for valuables, then began the transfer of prisoners and cargo. If the captured sloop was a fast one and he fancied the vessel, he kept it. If it was slow, he sank it.

The *Adventure*'s surgeon bound the wounds of his men, and the able-bodied seamen set about swabbing down the slippery bloody decks. The white heat that consumed him in battle gradually faded to be replaced by an almost sensual pleasure. With iron bar in hand, he smashed open barrels. It didn't matter to him that the blood of the other ship's crewmen streaked his clothes or that he had received cuts himself. He was oblivious to this as he pried up box lids, opened chests within them, and examined diamonds, gold coins, jewelry, and fine silks. By the time his crew had hauled up all the cargo from the hold of a plundered ship, the open crates, stove-in barrels, and goods strewn everywhere made the deck of *The Adventure* look and smell like a floating Eastern marketplace.

Today he shook his massive bearded head in frustration. Could a leopard changes his spots? No more than a man. What was he, Blackbeard, doing living in Bath, fifty miles from the coast, instead of spending his days on the high seas where he could find adventure. Not his girl-wife, Mary Ormond, nor any other wife had ever kept him away long from his beloved mistress—the sea.

Meanwhile the governor of Virginia was taking a serious interest in Blackbeard's presence off the North Carolina Outer Banks. Alexander Spotswood had convinced himself that there was imminent danger of Blackbeard leading a pirate invasion of Virginia; a less admirable reason for Spotswood's interest in the "former" pirate was his belief that Blackbeard possessed a vast treasure of gold, silver, and jewels and that the man who captured him, including the governor himself, would share the loot.

Spotswood rented two sloops with money out of his own pocket. Under the command of Lieutenant Robert Maynard and a man named Hyde, the *Pearl* and the *Ranger* set sail for Ocracoke Inlet on the morning of November twenty-first, the two armed vessels arriving at sunset.

Elated, Maynard saw the mast of *The Adventure* in the distance beyond the dunes. He would attack the next morning. He knew the pirate captain was unaware of his presence. Maintenance work on *The Adventure* and social life in Bath, however, had not kept the story of the ghost seaman from Blackbeard's thoughts.

Israel Hands had told the captain what he had heard. "Some says he was dressed all in black with a face fearsome as the Devil himself."

"The Devil, ay. Tell 'em they just met *me* roaming the deck at night, and they didn't know their own captain." Teach laughed uproariously.

"But captain, others saw horns 'a top his head and said his face and neck was drenched with blood—a horrid sight!"

"Rot!" bellowed Blackbeard in anger.

And now as he leaned arrogantly against the rail, he heard a sound . . . a sound that shouldn't be there. It was the rhythmic, barely perceptible sound of the dip of oars cutting the water.

There was more light now, and he raised his spy glass swiftly. A rowboat was approaching *The Adventure*, and behind it in the distance he saw the outlines of two large sloops. Black Caesar shouted the alert.

"When the rowboat comes in range, greet 'em with a round of shot," Blackbeard bellowed. The crashing thunder of *The Adventure's* guns reverberated across the water, and the rowboat scurried back to the protection of the sloops. It was then that Blackbeard made his decision.

He could have decided to flee for his crew was small, and the odds were heavily against him, but he was never a man to run from a fight. To the first mate's surprise the pirate suddenly seized the wheel from him and began steering *The Adventure* straight toward Ocracoke, as if to beach her, all the while his cannon maintaining a constant fire.

Blackbeard's men looked up from their guns in surprise. Quartermaster Thomas Miller dashed to the helm, seized Blackbeard by the shoulder, and pointed to the ever-nearing land. Blackbeard, holding the wheel in one hand, reached out with the other and without a word knocked Miller to the deck. By the time the stunned quartermaster scrambled to his feet, he had divined Blackbeard's plan.

Blackbeard, a master navigator in his home waters, had no intention of beaching his ship. He was steering *The Adventure* into a small uncharted channel with a sandbar that would separate the vessel from the two sloops. Within minutes the pursuing *Ranger* and the *Pearl* grounded themselves on the hidden sandbar.

Now they were within shouting distance. "Damn you for villains," Blackbeard roared at them. "Who are you, and where do you come from?"

"You can see by our flag we aren't pirates," retorted Maynard.

"Then come closer. Send your boat on board so that I can see who you are," demanded Blackbeard.

"I can't spare my boat, but I'll come aboard you with my sloop," Maynard called back.

Blackbeard felt a surge of excitement. The enemy was going to try to board *The Adventure* by force. At the same time he knew the sloops had more than twice the number of men he had—but he would fight.

"Damnation seize my soul if I give you any mercy or take any from you!" he bellowed across the water at Maynard. Then raising a bowl of rum, he tipped back his head and drank, roaring when he'd drunk his fill: "To the battle!"

"I expect no quarter from you nor shall I give any," shouted Maynard.

Taking advantage of the minutes before the two English sloops could dislodge themselves from the sandbar, Blackbeard ordered his gunner Phil Morton to train *The Adventure*'s cannons in a broadside on their attackers. Blackbeard signaled, and his eight cannons fired, leaving smoke hanging in the air. When the powerful guns fired, the force of the explosion jammed *The Adventure* back into the shoreline grounding her, but the pirates quickly re-floated her.

The cannon fire killed twenty-nine men outright on

the two Royal sloops. Hyde, captain of the *Pearl*, was dead, and Lieutenant Maynard's second and third officers were killed or badly wounded. With his one mighty volley Blackbeard had cut Maynard's forces by half. The *Ranger* was now disabled for combat.

The small crew of pirates boldly cast grappling irons over the rail of the *Pearl*. Blackbeard had his own surprise ready for the Royal Navy—hand grenades made from bottles filled with shot and fuses. He had used them before, and they created havoc on deck. Within minutes the British sloop *Pearl* was almost obscured by billowing smoke, and most of the crew appeared to be lying upon the deck.

"Board her and cut them to pieces," Blackbeard ordered exultantly. But, in desperation, Maynard had used an old trick of sea warfare, having men remain below until he gave them the signal to come up. To the pirate's surprise, men, weapons in hand, poured from the hold to meet them. Quickly realizing what had happened, Blackbeard shouted encouragement to his crew.

There had been no time for the men on the sloop to remove the men killed by the pirate ship's first volley, and the living battled on the deck in hand-to-hand combat among the bodies of the dead. In their midst Blackbeard wielded his great cutlass, cutting down men on every side of him. He had always sworn he would never be taken alive, and now he fought with the ferocity and courage of a lion.

At the height of the conflict Blackbeard and Maynard met face to face. Each pulled a pistol and fired. Blackbeard, rushed from all sides by Maynard's men, missed, but Maynard's bullet tore through the pirate's massive body. The pirate captain ignored it and battled furiously on. Now, only a few feet apart, they used their swords. Blackbeard delivered such a powerful blow that his cutlass blade slashed Maynard's sword off at the hilt. Maynard hurled the hilt wildly back at Blackbeard but was forced to withdraw and cock his pistol. Seizing his advantage, Blackbeard lunged toward him for the kill.

He whipped the blade of his cutlass high to gain the momentum for a mighty slash down through Maynard's body, but while the cutlass was still upraised, a British seaman came up behind Blackbeard and struck a blow that opened an enormous wound in his neck and throat. The seaman's thrust saved Maynard's life, for it delayed the movement of the pirate's cutlass, making it glide through the air before him almost in slow motion.

And it was then that Blackbeard saw a hideous sight. For the first time his men saw an expression of fear on his face. Reflected upon the gleaming metal was a huge head. It was the countenance of a hideous monster with peaked brows—the hair all matted and dripping blood—that hung suspended before him. The features were contorted with fury and the eyes glared with a rage like the fires of hell.

Later they said Blackbeard had finally recognized the "extra crewman" seen on the last voyage of *The Adventure*.

And it was the *Devil* !

❖   *Lieutenant Maynard arrived in Bath Town after the battle with the head of Blackbeard hanging from his sloop's bowsprit. The pirate captain had died with the courage of a lion after taking five pistol shots in his body and receiving twenty severe knife cuts. "Here was the end of that courageous brute who might have been a hero had he been fighting for a good cause," wrote a historian afterward.*

The General's Ghost

Upon the windswept sandy ramparts of Fort Fisher
the ghost of one of the South's
great generals still haunts the battlefield

Souh of Wilmington there is a peninsula of land
between the Cape Fear River and the Atlantic Ocean. The
distance between the river and the ocean gradually narrows,
and near the tip of the land where the highway ends are the
remains of Fort Fisher.

This is a haunted land. Mounds of sand with live oak
trees twisting among them mark what once was the "Gibraltar
of the Confederacy." On one side is the ocean and just beyond
the breakers. Sometimes at low tide the skeletons of blockade
runners can be seen. There should be many ghosts here. The
ghost of the Confederacy is one, for in a sense what happened
here made it die. Moreover, there should be the ghosts of
hundreds of men who fought and died in one of the most
savage hand-to-hand battles ever waged on this continent.

But the ghost seen here is that of a Confederate
general, one of the best the Confederacy had. He was William
Whiting, born in Mississippi, graduated first in his class at
West Point, and former commander of a division of the Army
of Northern Virginia.

Several years following the end of the War, a group of Confederate veterans who had served at Fort Fisher returned to visit the wrecked fort. They lingered longer than they had planned, recalling memories of the great battle and still blaming General Bragg for not coming to their aid. As the shadows stretched across the parapets they were startled to see the figure of a Confederate officer climbing to a gun emplacement on the land side of the fort where the old Wilmington road wandered through the trees to the fort entrance.

For a moment they thought another veteran had come to join them although they weren't expecting an officer dressed in Confederate uniform. They watched spellbound as the officer mounted the parapet, gazed in the direction of the old road, and then, as they started toward him, vanished.

Each one of the half dozen men knew what the others were thinking. It was the ghost of "Little Billy," as he had been affectionately called by the men who had known him.

For several moments there was silence and then one of the veterans said, "That's the same spot where he was wounded."

Another added, "It's a shame they had to take him to a prison up North to die."

On the trip back to Wilmington nothing else was said.

During the years of Reconstruction other veterans visited the fort. They didn't talk much about the ghost or what they saw there, but this is not uncommon with men after a war is over.

Today, if you go to Fort Fisher and you don't see the General in gray, it is not because he isn't there. If the wind is blowing in from the sea and the breakers are crashing over the timbers of the wrecked ships, you may not hear his footsteps. But wait until dusk and in the shadows of the fort you will sense he is nearby.

Let me tell you what happened there. All through the war Wilmington had been the favorite port for the blockade runners bringing in the supplies which the Confederacy so desperately needed and carrying cotton back to England to get the hard cash to hold the southern economy intact.

But as the war went on, the other ports of the Confederacy were closed one by one, either through capture by Union forces or the growing strength of the Union fleet. By the end of 1864 Wilmington was the only port left open between the Confederacy and the outside world, and it was protected by the "Gibraltar of the South," Fort Fisher.

The fort had been built out of sand, marsh grass, pine timbers, and the imagination and skill of its commanding officer, Colonel William Lamb. Colonel Lamb took command of the fort on July 4, 1862, when it "amounted to nothing" and two years later had a fort of such strength that the Union fleet dared not come too close to the entrance of the river. Happy were the blockade runners when they came within range of the fort's guns, for the pursuing Yankee ships were then forced to turn back.

Fort Fisher became such a problem for the Union that President Lincoln, pacing the corridors of the White House in Washington, finally made the ultimate decision—to send practically the entire Atlantic fleet and the best of his troops against it.

In December of '64 General Lee's aides brought word that the Union was gathering a great armada of ships to attack Fort Fisher. General Lee had written that so long as the port of Wilmington remained open his army had a chance. But Lee knew Colonel Lamb and his 36th North Carolina regiment stationed at the fort were no match for the force the Union was about to hurl against them.

Despite Lee's own shortage of troops, he immediately dispatched General Robert F. Hoke and six thousand of his veteran troops to Fort Fisher. These troops would be placed under the general command of the Department of Wilmington, which roughly embraced all the Confederate defenses along the river.

Unfortunately, Jefferson Davis, the Confederate president, chose this moment to send one of his favorite generals to take command of the area from General Whiting. Sentiment in the South was summed up by one line in a Richmond newspaper which said: "Bragg has been sent to command the troops at Wilmington—good-bye Wilmington."

The Union commander of the invasion fleet was also most unpopular in the South. General Benjamin Butler, called "Beast" Butler, landed his troops a few miles up the beach out of range of the guns of the fort. It was his plan after the mass shelling by the Union fleet to move his troops in and take the fort.

While the Union gunboats blazed incessantly at the fort, a young Confederate fell into the hands of Butler's pickets. The captured soldier casually mentioned that Hoke and his men were on their way to save the fort. Upon hearing this news, General Butler quickly surveyed the fort and decided his position was precarious. He immediately ordered a retreat back to the beach. Butler may not have been the first man off the beach but he was certainly not the last. His army left in such haste that they forgot an entire brigade, leaving it on the beach for the night.

In the morning, through the efforts of the navy, the brigade was rescued and Butler and his fleet returned North in humiliation.

General Bragg had staged an elaborate review of Hoke's troops for the citizens of Wilmington and then had ordered Hoke's men to "dig in" at a place called Sugar Loaf about eight miles up the peninsula. Bragg himself set up his headquarters at Sugar Loaf with Hoke and his men, several batteries of artillery, and about fifteen hundred North Carolina Reserves.

After the first attack on the fort failed, General Bragg congratulated both Whiting and Lamb for their successful defense. However, these same officers were not lulled into apathy by the praise of the commanding general. They appealed for more guns, men, and ammunition. Lamb and Whiting knew the Federals would be back with more men and ships for another try. General Bragg did not agree.

Lincoln replaced Butler with a competent general and on January 12, 1865, Colonel Lamb mounted the ramparts of his fort and saw "the most formidable fleet that ever floated on the sea" supplemented by transports carrying eighty-five hundred men. This time the fleet began an immediate and intense bombardment of the fort which in the colonel's words was "beyond description." The bombardment continued day and night. The Confederates, short of gunpowder and shells, were ordered by Lamb to fire each gun only once every half hour.

When it became apparent to Whiting that Bragg was not going to strongly reinforce the fort but remain at Sugar Loaf with his Army, General Whiting commandeered a ship and sailed down the river to Fort Fisher alone. Walking through the bursting shells, he entered the fort and found Colonel Lamb at his post. Above the roar of the guns he shouted to the colonel, "Lamb, my boy, I have come to share your fate. You and your garrison are to be sacrificed."

Lamb could not believe Bragg would desert him and asked, "Where are Hoke's men?" Whiting replied that when he left Headquarters, General Bragg had just issued orders for removing his stores and ammunition and was "looking for a place to fall back upon."

The Federal troops poured ashore on the beach far enough north to be out of range of the fort's guns. As the blue regiments formed and began their advance Whiting telegraphed an urgent message to Bragg:

"The enemy are about to assault; they outnumber us heavily. We are just manning our parapets. Fleet has extended down the sea front outside and firing heavily. Enemy on the beach in front of us in very heavy force, not more than seven hundred yards from us. Nearly all land guns disabled. Attack! Attack! It is all I can say and all you can do."

In response to this appeal Bragg dispatched what he said was "eleven hundred veteran infantry" down the river by steamer. The ships were fired upon heavily by the Federal guns and less than half the men reached the fort. Colonel Lamb put the figure at three hundred and fifty South Carolinians of Johnson Hagood's brigade. Unfortunately, the troops had to run a half-mile under the naval bombardment from the Union guns. They reached the fort out of breath and Colonel Lamb immediately sent them to an old bomb shelter to rest. This was the last help Lamb was to receive.

All at once the great Union fleet stopped firing and blew their steam whistles. It was the signal for the final attack. At the point where the land and sea faces of the fort joined overlooking the beach, several thousand Union marines and sailors charged. Lamb with a few hundred of his men threw them back in a fierce hand-to-hand fight. Just as it appeared this attack was over, three Federal battle flags appeared on the ramparts of the fort to the west. Eight thousand Federal troops followed these flags.

Both Whiting and Lamb gathered what men were left and launched a counterattack. The fighting swirled from gun emplacement to gun emplacement. In the smoke and roar of battle a Union officer shouted to Whiting to surrender. "Go to hell!" Whiting replied. A moment later he sank to the sand mortally wounded. Colonel Lamb, fighting on with a few hundred of his men, was also wounded and the command fell to Major James Reilly, who made the final stand at the last gun emplacement.

General Whiting was taken prisoner and, despite his wounds, was taken to a Union prison on Governor's Island in New York harbor where he died a short time later.

The spot where Whiting fell in the battle is unmarked, but go to Fort Fisher at dusk and listen to the wind and the waves and you may find that the gray-clad figure of the Confederate general still lingers there.

❖ *The area now is part of a state historic site.*

The Whaler's Return

He wondered with a frightened, empty
feeling if she had married

Most seafaring men have their superstitious side, and so did Edward Pond. But he had no premonitions when his ship headed out to sea from its home port at Stonington, Connecticut.

His heavily muscled arms and rough, scarred hands were used to hard work for he had been a whaler for some thirty years before signing on with the crew of the *Charles Sprague*. Pond was unusually happy about this voyage just before Thanksgiving in 1886. The *Sprague* was a fine new three-masted schooner with a long quarterdeck. His only son would be serving with him as third mate—the first time they had ever sailed together.

On board he watched the boy with pride. A tall blond young man, Sylvester Pond was born and raised to go to sea. Only twenty, he had a keen eye for how a sail should be bent and a strong, skilled forearm that could make a coil of rope leap and twist like a writhing snake.

They were only a few days out of Stonington when a moderate chop began, but it was hardly felt in a vessel like the *Sprague*. The crew awakened to hear rain pelting the deck and every direction was a curtain of gray. The sun did not rise that day. By afternoon the schooner *Sprague* was hurtling down the side of one mountainous wave and up another, scudding before the storm.

Father and son were both on deck when it happened. In one billowing black onslaught the sea boarded the ship! Veteran whaler Edward Pond looked up to see a wall of water high as a tidal wave. Suddenly he became a tiny particle of humanity encased in unbearably heavy wetness, unable to breathe, propelled through endless reaches of blackness with momentum so great he thought it would strip off his very flesh.

His chest was ready to burst, the pressure in his ears was excruciating, and he was almost unconscious when, with tremendous impact, the water hurled him against the side of the cabin. Seconds later a yawl, its davit broken, smote him with such cruel violence that it crushed his limp body against the cabin wall.

Sylvester managed to reach his father while he still lived and release him. He took his father to a bunk and arranged pillows around his bruised and broken body, but mercifully Edward Pond never regained consciousness. Five hours later, with his son's arms around him, he died.

The fourth day of the storm was Thanksgiving, and the tempest raged on, the *Sprague* scudding helplessly before hurricane-force winds. About midday a monstrous wave reached up from the tumult of foam and blackness below to seize and crush the vessel. In a second of horror Sylvester Pond saw the towering gray-green wall of water looming high above his head and knew he was doomed.

The water crashed down upon him with stunning force and swept him from the deck into the seething black cauldron below. He fought to come up, reached the surface, only to have the icy arm of a wave push him down again. His body grew numb from cold—his will to live was fast ebbing when he was lifted up in the grip of another mountainous wave, pulled under, battered, swept on with the sand of the shore scraping his flesh raw, and then, miraculously, tossed upon the beach.

The place where the limp, sodden body of Sylvester Pond lay was a narrow golden spit of sand off the North Carolina coast called Shackleford Banks. When he finally opened his eyes he was being cared for in the modest cottage of a fisherman, and it was not until the second day that he felt strong enough to talk.

"My shipmates? Are they alive?" he breathed weakly.

"Aye, almost all of them," replied John Chadwick. "We're taking care of them here at Diamond City."

"And my ship—still afloat?"

Chadwick nodded and Sylvester, spent from his ordeal, fell asleep once more. John Chadwick looked over at his wife and shook his head.

"He will have a long wait before he's fit to set sail on a whaling voyage again," said she. "What about the vessel?"

"They're towing the ship into the bight to repair her. None can say when she will be seaworthy for the mizzenmast lies broken in half across her deck."

There were good shipwrights at Cape Lookout, but no tall, strong trees. The problem would be to replace a timber the size of the Sprague's huge mizzenmast.

Like Pond, the first Chadwick was a New England whaler. During the 1700s the Chadwick men had lived in whalers' huts on Shackleford Banks. Most whalers stayed for the season but the Chadwicks came back to settle. When the

New England men who came down for whaling went out to sea to search for whales, the islanders watched, and then stopped waiting for providence to wash the whales ashore. They boated out themselves, harpoons held high, to hunt the animals down.

John Chadwick was a tall rangy man with a sun-burned, heavily lined broad face and bright blue eyes. He was also a good man, and he and his wife were soon treating Sylvester as they would have a son. Sylvester Pond would have been dead of exposure had he not been quickly found. His body was battered and abraded from the sand and he was painfully weak. "He may get the pneumonia, you know, John," warned Ann Chadwick, but the young man was fortunate, and with the couple's good care, each day he grew stronger.

At the end of the second week Chadwick told him, "you've been in the house too much, lad. It's a taste of the good salt air ye need and a stroll about the island. You'll want to thank Joe Etheridge, the keeper of the lifesaving station. 'Twas Joe who found you on Thanksgiving Day."

"I can't remember it."

"I'm not surprised. He said you were stretched out on the sand limp as a piece 'a seaweed, an' he took you for dead." Mrs. Chadwick's gray eyes were moist.

Sylvester Pond soon knew everything about Diamond City on the eastern end of Shackleford Banks all the way to within the shadow of Cape Lookout Lighthouse. Only the year before, Joe Etheridge had named the community for the unusual diamond pattern which made the lighthouse the most prominent landmark for miles.

Chadwick took him on his own daily rounds over the island, and Sylvester became familiar with the few stores, the factory to extract oil from porpoises, the oyster house, the small crab packing plant, and the church. A town of about five hundred people, Diamond City covered half of Shackleford Banks and melted into a community called Wade's Shore.

Although it was now mid-December, the days were mild, for here, south of Cape Hatteras, temperatures were warmed by the Gulf Stream flowing up from the south. Shackleford Banks, where Pond now found himself, was one of a string of narrow barrier islands off the North Carolina coast and was separated from the mainland by shallow sounds.

Created by narrow, ribbonlike patterns of ocean beaches, sand dunes, luxuriant forests, and salt marshes, islands like Shackleford extended along the coast for several hundred miles. This world inhabited by Chadwick and the others Bankers, as the natives of the Outer Banks islands were called, was tranquil, but it was also a place of strong winds, blowing sand, and glaring sun drenching the sand dunes, green meadows, and marshes.

Sylvester had spent his live on the coast of New England. He was at home on the busy streets of Stonington and he loved the noisy docks ripe with the odors of fish, spices, and citrus fruit from the tropics. He had watched the slave ships washed down before they went back to Africa for another black cargo and seen the loading of flour, barrelled beef, pork, and other commodities heading out for Jamaica and Barbados. It was a bustling port. Unlike the people of the Outer Banks, he had never really lived close to nature.

While he was regaining his strength, he and Chadwick took long walks through the half-light of the island's forest of myrtle, pine, dogwood, oak, and cedar. One day, at the forest's edge, he gazed out over a grassy meadow at a wild pony, and its soft brown eyes stared back at him unafraid.

Sylvester was fascinated. "I've heard these ponies descended from Spanish horses."

"Yep. Swam ashore from ships wrecked off the Cape."

The two men knelt down and, thrusting cupped hands into the water, they drank from one of the small fresh-water ponds. Sylvester grimaced. His mouth rebelled at the rotten-egg taste that came from the marsh grass giving off hydrogen sulfide to flavor the water on most of the islands.

They climbed sand dunes covered with thickets and shrubs. A cottontail rabbit streaked off, and a startled cat-bird feeding in wind-twisted trees emitted its peculiar squall. They plodded through soft, coarse sand mixed with broken bits of shell, and Sylvester realized he had not fully regained his strength.

Once there was a frenzied screeching and fluttering of wings all around them. They were surrounded by a dark cloud of birds, and Sylvester covered his face with his arms until the beating wings had fled. They had disturbed nesting terns.

Beyond the dunes the sea was calm and blue and he could see a necklace of mullet fishermen pulling in their long net filled with a shimmering silver treasure of fish. The bearded young seaman began to experience a sense of peace. Here there was no hurry, but time for everything.

At first the quiet and absence of bustle, the lack of concern over the passage of time frustrated him, but gradually a subtle change came about in the New Englander. He waked each morning, and if the weather was gray and rainy, he accepted it and busied himself mending nets, caulking Chadwick's boat, or feeding livestock. There was always something to be done.

He read the large family Bible, one of the few books owned by the Chadwicks, and he became absorbed in the art of scrimshaw, carving intricate designs on the whale bones he picked upon the beach. He chafed less often at the enforced shaping of his days and began to share the attitude of the

Outer Bankers, accepting the reality that his life was entirely in the hands of nature and governed by its moods.

But during the evenings, Pond sometimes grew restive. There was little diversion save a Saturday night gathering in one of the homes or a church social.

"You need to go over to the church and get yourself a box supper and a pretty girl to walk home," John Chadwick advised.

"What if she won't let a stranger like me walk her home?"

"Then I'll vouch for you."

Saturday night Sylvester and some of his fellow seamen gathered at the small unpainted church. He stared around him at all the shy-looking girls standing stiffly holding the box suppers they had brought. Not one appealed to him, and he attempted to leave but John Chadwick fixed him with a stern eye: "No, ye don't."

At that moment a slender girl in a dress the color of pale green sea water slipped in the side door of the church. Her hair was dark and shiny with patches of gold where the sun had gilded it. Chadwick saw him looking at the girl.

"What's her name?"

"Virginia Davis and her box supper will go for a handsome price."

Most of the suppers had been put up for bid and purchased by now but not Virginia's. Sylvester felt encouraged for there were only a few men left to bid on the remaining boxes. Then the auctioneer intoned loudly, "What am I bid for Miss Virginia's supper? It's bound to be a fine meal!" Three young men began the bidding and then there were two—Sylvester and a heavy-set young fellow named Myers. He had an arrogant, almost brutal face and Pond took an instant dislike to him. Myers made an inordinately high bid and Sylvester topped it. Sylvester saw him start to bid again but apparently change his mind and remain silent.

To Sylvester's surprise the girl looked over at him and frowned but the box was his and he intended to claim the privilege of sitting with her. He walked over to her table and introduced himself. At first she was quite shy. There were few visitors to the island and Sylvester was an outsider. She treated him coolly as they began eating, but when Sylvester spoke of his liking for the Banks, she was pleased and asked him about New England. He soon found himself attracted by her warmth and interest in his stories of his boyhood, while a short distance away, the disappointed Myers sat glowering at them.

Just after eight they left the church and started off on the path to her home. They had walked only a short distance when Sylvester heard the brush crackle ahead of them and out stepped James Myers, blocking their way. Sylvester felt his face flush with anger.

"You're a bad loser aren't you, Myers?"

"Hush!" said Virginia. "What do you mean by following me like this, James?"

"You want this greasy whaler to walk you home?"

Sylvester moved toward him threateningly, but Virginia put a restraining hand on his arm.

"He bought my box supper, and he has the right to walk me home. Let us by, please."

Myers looked furious but he stepped to one side.

From that day on, Sylvester and Virginia often walked the island together. He marveled at the strangely beautiful skeletons of trees killed by the advancing sand and spray, still standing in eerie ghost forests on the ocean side while the forest continued to advance on the growing side of the island. The dunes at Shackleford were the largest on the southeastern coast. The young people played upon them like two children, hiding, climbing, tumbling down into the soft sand below—and sometimes embracing.

Together they watched the antics of the loons, the cormorants, the swans, and the sea ducks. Occasionally an arctic auk would wheel above them, and when it did, Sylvester said nothing but his heart lurched at the sight of that bird, so familiar, and his thoughts turned toward the great whales of the arctic.

The days passed swiftly. Whether he was in love or not, Sylvester scarcely knew. The young women in the life of this tall, blond-haired, blue-eyed whaler, still more boy than man at twenty, had been few. To him, the most important "she" had always been a ship or the sea.

Finally, in late January, he watched the mizzenmast being towed in behind a boat from Florida. As John Chadwick had predicted, it had taken time. A ninety-foot-tall straight pine had to be located at a shipbuilding company and then hauled up the coast. Even in an area with tall trees, it had been a long search to find the right one. Meanwhile, bad weather had set in at Cape Lookout. Sylvester and the crewmen were restless, and in New England the owners of the ship fretted about the money they were losing each day during the long wait.

When the mizzenmast was finally pulled into the bight, it needed to be lashed to the dock until it was time to raise her. Meanwhile the Captain was signing on new crewmen to replace those injured or drowned in the storm, those who had wandered off, and the one who had married and swore he would go to sea no more. The Captain swore, too, saying he would use muscle, if necessary, to get everyone back aboard, and his threat was all that held in line some of the more timid seamen who had not forgotten the Thanksgiving storm.

Crewmen and islanders watched the lifting of the four-ton mast. A tripod was used to attach and unattach the line as needed while the piece was guided and positioned. Precision and skill were essential for there was always the danger that the mast would crash on the men.

Ropes were adjusted and the immense tree trunk was rising slowly in the air while ant-sized men on the beach below stood ready to guide the piece in. Suddenly, a rope snapped! The tree swayed and leaned abruptly as though it would topple, but the other ropes held. Everyone sighed with relief.

While Sylvester continued to watch tensely, the broken rope was replaced and work was over for the day. Tomorrow the small, one-ton mizzen-topmast would go up and then the vessel would be ready.

But morning brought rain and wind from the southeast and for several days there was no let up in the weather. By the time the Southeaster had passed, two of the most experienced shipwrights had disappeared and there was more delay, much to the impatience of the New England ship owners.

Sylvester was no longer in any great hurry. Not only was he seeing Virginia often, but here there was a season, and the sea determined that season. He was warmed by the sun, delayed by the wind, slowed by heavy fog, and he had come to accept these postponements calmly.

When he returned one day from watching the slow progress on the ship, he found John Chadwick absorbed in the sharpening of his whaling lance. It was a three-foot steel shaft on an eight-foot pole and Sylvester sat looking on. He desperately wanted to go, for he loved the excitement of whaling. Surely, his friend would ask him. Chadwick continued working on his lance for most of the afternoon but seemed little inclined to talk. Now and then he would examine the point, give a slight smile of satisfaction as he touched it, and then continue his sharpening.

"Going whaling, eh?" Sylvester finally asked.

"Aye."

"Near Little River?"

"We'll set up a crow's nest on one of the sandhills between there and the Cape."

"I guess those goin'll be the Lewises, the Guthries, the Moores . . . . "

"If you're gettin' round to askin' will there be a space for another man, there will," broke in John. "Come on. We'll get you a lance."

"But I need a harpoon," said Sylvester boldly.

Chadwick gave him a quizzical look but did not reply. It took a special kind of man—brawny, with a keen eye, unerring aim, and the boldness to throw his harpoon the split second the whale was in the right position.

When they reached the beach three six-man crews were being made up. Chadwick joined four men and Pond made the sixth, as if it were meant to be. He was given a lance from the equipment house, but Chadwick did not give him a harpoon. If a whale was sighted the men would leap into their boat, and the whale belonged to the crew that reached it first. They always went in at least two boats so that if one was overturned, the other could help.

While the men waited they talked of previous years and whales they had caught, calling each whale by a name they had given it. There was the "Mayflower" and "Tom Rose's Whale" and "Cap'n Jody's," and they would recall how one of their number had drowned or how hard a whale had fought. Despite the relaxed talk there was an underlying tension. Fishermen had reported signs that meant whales were nearby. They had seen bits of floating cuttlefish indicating whales high in the water feeding at the surface.

For the first time, Sylvester would be chasing the right whale, an animal which inhabited waters close to island clusters. He recalled a warning he had often heard: "Beware of a sperm's jaws and a right whale's flukes." Both had proved deadly for many a whaler.

He longed for his own harpoon, but all he had been given was a lance, so he began to rehearse in his mind what he would do. Standing in the bow of the pilot boat, the harpooner would wait until he was in the most favorable position to strike. The first harpoon must be followed by the second almost immediately. At the instant when the crew thought the whale would surface, they would haul the line in hard and come up right beside the whale.

Then it would be up to him to strike swiftly with his long, sharp, leaded lance, piercing the whale's most vital spot and then withdrawing the lance. If he were fortunate, he might slay the leviathan with a single blow.

His thoughts were interrupted by a loud cry from the lookout on the dunes. "Thar she blows!" And out at sea he saw the characteristic spout of the right whale. It was a double V-shaped blast of misty white water ascending fifteen feet in the air from the creature's two nostrils.

"Thar again!" came the excited shout of the lookout as the crews were jumping into the boats. Chadwick manned the foremost oar, his harpoon at his side. The harpoon was attached to an extremely strong tarred hemp line. They shoved off just behind the other boat, surrounded by the salt spray from the breakers and the smell of the sea. If the whale had been frightened by the sound of the shouts from the beach, Sylvester knew he might dive for as long as twenty minutes. But the animal did not do so. Out among the waves

Sylvester saw the double white plumes of the V-shaped blow rise high above the water.

All was quiet. The men made no sound, as whales have acute hearing. They were less than half a mile from their prey now and they paddled the boats furiously in the direction of the twin spouts. Then they sighted other puffs of vapor, smokelike wisps hovering over the gray water, and beneath the wisps the surface of the water churned and shifted. It was toward this spot of turbulent air and water that the two small boats headed, buoyant and graceful, leaping from billow to billow.

"Pull, boys, pull," exhorted Chadwick in a voice so low it was only a whisper above the sounds of the sea. The boats hurtled on toward their prey. Sylvester's heart pounded. Vapor had now become jets and seemed to be all around them—there were two whales, not one! Sylvester saw the harpooner in the boat ahead of him stand up, and after an interminable moment he watched the long black dart fly through the air toward the shoulder of one of the whales.

The harpooner's boat rose into the air and, to Sylvester Pond's horror, the whale rose with it and two gushes of vapor shot up. Men and oars flew in every direction into the water. Then the small craft fell back in the trough of a wave. Though partially filled with water, it was still afloat and the men began to scramble back into it. The harpooner had only grazed the whale and the whale had surfaced briefly before making a deep dive.

Sylvester turned to see the other whale beside the boat he shared with Chadwick. Chadwick was waiting until the instant came when he was in the most favorable position to strike. Now it came. Hurling the harpoon, he fastened it solid in the whale's flesh, and their boat took off like a streak.

Its bow soared above the water—leapt across the waves as the animal raced on, pulling the boat after him.

Chadwick turned and signaled Sylvester to change places. Sylvester was filled with excitement. He was to deliver the mortal blow with his lance as soon as they could draw close enough to the whale. He positioned himself.

It will be dead whale or stove boat, he thought as their small craft began to gain on the giant of the sea. It had to be a dead whale. He would see to it. Now it was "wood and black skin"—the whale was touching their boat!

Sylvester raised his arm and with all his strength he plunged his lance into the dark mass beside the boat. A tremendous, shuddering impact went through his body, and, quickly, with a hard upward tug, he managed to withdraw the lance. Soon they were surrounded by a crimson sea, and Sylvester felt shaken by the whole experience. The whale appeared to be dying but soon the animal sped off again, and once more the captors became the captives as the whale towed them at breakneck speed, lashing the waves with his great tail. They rode through the mist of a cloud of spray until gradually the boat slowed. At last death had arrived, and the leviathan was still.

With the help of the other boat, they towed the whale to shore. Sylvester's arms tugged at his oar. He still felt the tension that would ebb from his mind and body slowly—the excitement of the chase and a second-by-second matching of wits with the whale. He wished he could care more about the money that would come later, but even while he was absorbed in the necessary "cutting in" and "trying out" which produced the valuable clear barrels of oil, he was reliving the chase. Old men gathered around the crewmen as they worked, telling their own tales of whales that once had been.

Did he want to sign on a whaling ship? Sylvester knew a year or more was not an unusual length of time for a whaler to be away from his home port, but sometimes it was twice that long. He thought of Virginia Davis. The *Charles Sprague* was almost ready to sail.

It awaited the positioning of the mizzen-topmast which must be expertly handled as it was fitted in the hounds, the hole in the large wooden collar atop the mizzen-mast. The collar would hold the heavy topmast firmly in place. Two men stood on the collar and, as everyone watched, they began to guide the tall topmast into the hounds. Death could be the result if they should miss. On the ground another two men carefully held the great ropes, waiting for signals from above.

As the heavy topmast slid into the hole, the men on the collar pushed a massive wooden pin through to secure it and there was a cheer from the crowd. The crew began to load bags and barrels of sweet potatoes, salt pork, fresh water, and hardtack on board, and the next morning at sunrise the *Sprague* was only a black dot on the horizon. Sylvester Pond was on board, drawn by the magnet of faraway places and more whaling. He would go with the other whalers to Spritzenburg. He would hunt down whatever right whales were left to be hunted across the Arctic.

Some of his letters to Virginia were like the promises of a drinking man. "I'm swearing off whales, and this will be my last voyage," he would tell her, but that would be when week after week went by and no whales were sighted. It was then he would write of his longing to be back with her on the Outer Banks and how he would return and settle down forever.

When she didn't hear from him for a time, she knew the whalers were successful, and finally a letter would arrive, hastily scrawled, filled with the story of the chase. Page after page, she would pour over the words, so laden with excitement that she could hear the whales deep sonorous screams and the hoarse shouts of the men in the boats.

It's in the marrow of his bones, she would think. He will follow the whales wherever they go in their migrations, and he will never settle down to the life of an Outer Banker. The men on her island were shore-based whalers during the season, then the rest of the year they engaged in the quiet occupation of mullet fishing.

Four years went by until Sylvester Pond sailed into Cape Lookout Bight once more. There was little of the boy to be seen in the muscular, broad-shouldered young man. He disembarked from the small cargo vessel whose captain had agreed to put into Shackleford Banks for some barrels of the fine quality salt mullet produced in the area.

It was a warm July afternoon as he walked down the path beside the dunes toward Virginia's home hoping she would be there, anticipating how she would look when she saw him.

But there was no answer at the front door of the Davis home and he thought she must be at the summer church camp on the island. Then he had a deep sense of dread. He wondered with a frightened, empty feeling if she had married.

Should he go to the village and ask? He walked around thinking he would drink from the pump at the rear of the house. And then he saw her in the garden. She had her back turned. It had been four long years. Would there be a ring already on her finger? Her long hair rippled down to her waist, brown with the same tawny flecks of gold he remembered. His apprehension was so great that he was unable to speak.

Finally she turned, looked at him, and smiled. In that smile he read his future.

Like his friend Chadwick, and many a New Englander before him, he would adapt to the way of life here on the Banks. There would be quiet months of fishing in the bight or banding together with other fishermen to work the mullet nets at dawn.

Sylvester Pond would look forward to the shore whaling in the spring—but he would never put to sea on a whaler again.

❖   *This is a true story told by a member of the family of how Sylvester Pond, found unconscious on the beach after a shipwreck near Cape Lookout Lighthouse, later returned to the island to marry Virginia Davis. New blood has come to these remote islands with every shipwreck, whaling sloop, and war.*

The Unearthly Music of Roan Mountain

Go to the top if
you would hear its awesome sound

Once upon a time there was a man who had all of the things most men spend themselves for.

First of all he could number among his list of acquaintances many of the most famous men of his day. Why, at any moment, even here in the fashionable seclusion of his mountain home, the phone might ring. And the voice of a publisher, politician, or other prominent friend would come warmly over the wires seeking him out.

A writer such as he had much to contribute, especially now that his position in the literary world was secure. His most prosaic utterances were received as conversational gems. Even his physical presence was a contribution in the eyes of many. For certainly such a distinguished guest enhanced his host's prestige. And unsure of personal worth, how much better to huddle close to those who have arrived.

Lamotte Duval, and we will call him that to save possible embarrassment, had been everywhere. Just a casual reference to the countries he had visited was bound to impress. It had all been most exciting until he began to notice that hungry children were the same whether they begged on the streets of India or sat apathetically on the steps of a sharecropper's house and that the stench of poverty was as strong in the New York slums as in those of Morocco.

The time he had sought the most avaricious face which he could find to describe, the man he had found was not among the gamblers at Monte Carlo—but among his own circle in the exclusive apartment house where he spent most of his winters.

A vague dissatisfaction, the cause of which he could scarcely come to grips with, had become Duval's most frequent companion of late. He sat now in a comfortable chair facing a huge expanse of plate glass which overlooked one of the most gorgeous views in the North Carolina mountains.

In some towns standing might depend on a grandfather, an address at the top of the hill, or a certain street name. But here one of the most important symbols of status was "the view." And, of course, Lamotte Duval had it. In fact, what did he not have? On his magazine table were expensive and exquisitely done publications—a tribute to his taste. His bookshelves were lined with rare incunabula and first editions.

And now he was faced with deciding how and where he was to spend his summer. Should it be here in the mountains or would he really prefer listening to Wagner in Bayreuth, with an apartment for the summer at the Kronberg Castle near Frankfurt and perhaps a jaunt to the Olympic games?

Ten years ago he might have savored all this to the utmost. But ever so gradually a serpent had insinuated itself into this paradise and all but ruined his capacity to enjoy it. And just what was this viper? He didn't know himself. Ah, if it had been a man of more talent, superior intellect, whose work rivaled his own, he could have adjusted to that. For he had come to accept, nay even to thoroughly appreciate, the genius of other men.

Long years ago he had renounced that illusory and prideful struggle for recognition by the world as the "best" writer. Duval had been content to work diligently developing his own unique talent while tasting the not inconsiderable fruits of his labors.

But now an honest and incisive mind had finally turned itself inward. And the picture which Duval was beginning to see of himself and his life was not altogether pleasing. Although he had regarded religion with amused tolerance for the greatest part of his life, it how began to appear to him that this "myth of the masses" which he had failed to pursue had somehow begun to pursue him.

If he casually fingered a book it would turn out to be by Fénelon or perhaps Thomas à Kempis. And often it seemed that even the most impersonally begun conversation would turn toward religion. But the phenomena in the book of mountain stories he was now reading were clearly of scientific origin. As long as he was here so close to the locale he owed it to himself to investigate.

"The ghostly choir of Roan Mountain" some of the natives called it. Roan Mountain was not a long drive, and Lamotte read with fascination that on this mile-high plateau an awesome sound like wildly beautiful music had first been heard by herdsmen. This was as far back as the 1700s. When they told the story in the valley they spoke of hearing "a choir of angels."

As they talked the heads of the mountain folk nodded, for hadn't some venturesome souls been caught on the Roan in a thunderstorm and seen a circular rainbow? And if God wore a halo would it not be just such a rainbow? Anything could happen atop the Roan.

Here Lamotte Duval smiled at such naivety. For he had been to many faraway lands but never in any of them had he seen even one magic place. And yet at the thought of magic places some long-buried emotion of his youth stirred faintly within him. He read on about John Strother, a member of a boundary surveying commission back in 1799. In his diary Strother had written: "There is no shrubbery growing on the top of this mountain for several miles, and the wind has such power on top of this mountain that the ground is blowed in deep holes all over the northwest side."

And then in 1878 Colonel John Wilder heard the music as it had been heard a century before by the herdsmen. He built a summer hotel on the Roan and passed the story along to many an interested guest.

Among those who heard of it was a young scientist from Knoxville, Tennessee, named Henry E. Colton. Colton returned home to publish a treatise. Lamotte Duval read Colton's conclusions avidly.

"Several of the cattle tenders on the mountain and also Colonel Wilder had spoken to us about what they called 'Mountain Music,'" Colton wrote. "One evening they said it was sounding loud and Dr. D. P. Boynton of Knoxville, Hon. J. M. Thornburg and myself accompanied General Wilder to the glen to hear it. The sound was very plain to the ear. It was always loudest and most prolonged just after there would be a thunderstorm in either valley or one passing over the mountain. I used every argument I could to persuade myself that it simply was a result of some common cause and to shake the faith of the country people in its mysterious origin." They continued believing that the music came from angels. "But I only convinced myself that it was the result from two currents of air meeting each other in the suck between the two peaks where there was no obstruction of trees, one containing a greater, the other a lesser amount of electricity."

Here Lamotte Duval put down the book with sudden decision. This very afternoon he would learn the truth for himself. He noted the black clouds overhead. An occasional raindrop made a shiny little path as it slid down the outside of the wall of glass before him. Without waiting for his resolve to waver he strode out of the house and, getting into his small foreign-make car, headed toward Roan Mountain.

When he reached the mountain he drove almost to its top, parked his car, and began walking toward the crest of the plateau. In a few minutes he saw a line of rocks which he guessed to be where the foundation of Colonel John Wilder's hotel had been. By now the rain was a steady downpour beating against his face with almost primeval force. Stumbling, he caught himself at the edge of a rocky promontory and decided to take shelter under its overhang.

For almost a half hour he sat there waiting for the rain to stop, soaked to the skin. As he rested he began to berate himself for his foolishness, for there was certainly no music of any kind to be heard—only the pounding of the torrential rain.

Then as he strained to hear the slightest unusual noise his ears caught a faint sound. The rain stopped as if at the signal of some unseen hand and the sun drifted brilliantly from behind a cloud. Then he heard the sound again and more clearly. Gradually it gained in intensity, and what had first seemed to him to be merely the wind took on new tones like a choir of many voices. Wildly sweet, it built up to a shattering crescendo of sound which caught him up and flowed over him.

He listened incredulously, forgetting his damp discomfort. As he did so something indescribable began to take place within Lamotte Duval. Oriental women of old bound their feet, and so had the world placed fetter after fetter around Duval's spirit. Now it seemed as if one by one they were being unwound and swept away.

Finally all was quiet and Lamotte Duval, emotionally exhausted and utterly bewildered by the fierce beauty of the music, still made no move to rise. Then he climbed cautiously back upon the rocks above him. His eyes searched the sky for more storm clouds. They had completely disappeared, but to his astonishment there was something else in their place.

At the edge of the plateau was the most gorgeous rainbow he had ever beheld. Blue, yellow, pale green, and cerise, it shimmered high in the sky. And what was most amazing of all, the rainbow formed a complete circle! He remembered the words "God's halo," and as he did so his lips tried to form a smile. But they could not.

He clutched desperately at the last shreds of his skepticism. But they melted away. As he stood there gazing in wonderment he began to be aware of a new sensation. Somehow he felt as new and clean as he had as a boy. Duval watched the rainbow's glory until it faded into the sky and then, turning reluctantly, started back to his car.

When he reached home he was just in time to hear the insistent ring—ring—ring of his phone. But it could as easily have been ringing in another world on another planet. For Lamotte Duval smiled faintly and, heeding it not at all, walked over to his table by the window.

The book which he picked up and opened was just what he had thought it would be—*The Imitation of Christ* by Thomas à Kempis.

Lifesaver
of the Outer Banks

The testing of Malachi Corbel

A solitary figure wrapped in evening mist strode near the edge of the foaming surf. Strong easterly winds tugged at the brim of his oilskin hat, secured by a loop of cord under his jutting chin. Occasionally he looked up and studied the leaden sky.

Malachi Corbel had battled many a storm, and he had come to see each as having its own distinctive personality. The behavior of some storms might be tenacious, trying a man's patience to the limit. The ways of others were deceptive. They would seem to pass on, only to turn back and strike again with renewed savagery.

And then there were those storms so fierce, so vengeful that he was convinced they were incarnations of the Devil. This one was sending advance signals that a worthy adversary was on the way. He gazed up at the dark thunderheads massing in the sky, saw the gun-metal hue of the sea and the height of the waves.

Two storm petrels skittered over the water, their faint, piercing bird cries barely audible over the roar and crash of the breakers. He shivered slightly. He was not a superstitious man, but ever since his boyhood he had heard that the sight of petrels was a bad omen.

A short, heavily muscled man with piercing blue eyes and black curly hair streaked with gray, Malachi Corbel was Keeper of Wash Woods, the lifesaving station farthest to the north on the hazardous North Carolina coast. It was October 23, 1889, and a fine rain had started about midday.

He strained his eyes seaward. He knew that out there by now the winds had reached gale force. Vessels would be driven helplessly up the flanks of waves the size of small mountains, then plunge precariously, out of control, into the deep, wet valleys of the sea. Drenched men with rain lashing their faces would be shouting desperate commands, striving to be heard above the indescribable sound of the wind's fury. They would be clinging to the rails and fighting to keep from going overboard as tons of black water swept across the decks.

God help the luckless sloop that was blown upon treacherous Pebble Shoals, Corbel thought. Close beneath the surface of the water near the boundary line of Virginia and North Carolina, those grinding jaws lay hungrily in wait for their victims, and the jaws were often fed.

That evening Corbel went back to the station, boiled some coffee, and sat down to make an entry in his journal. Then he dozed until Waterfield and White came in from patrol duty.

"We spotted a light near the tip of the shoals," Waterfield reported. "Flashed our red signal but got no flash in reply."

Torrential rain pounded the roof of the lifesaving station, streaming down in crooked rivulets over the windows. Evans came in just before daybreak with some news.

"There's a vessel sunk to the north and its wreckage is floating ashore."

Keeper and crewmen hurriedly gulped coffee, jerked their oilskins on, and went out. Leaning into the force of the gale, they headed north toward Pebble Shoals, dragging a lifeboat behind them. The boat carried a Lyle gun. It was possible the wreck might be near enough to shoot the projectile and catch the vessel so that they could haul survivors to safety.

Along with slickers they wore hip boots, for the water was rising. As they approached the southern tip of the shoals, the dim outline of a ship's rigging loomed out of the mist and rain. They stared at what first appeared to be knots of tangled sails, and then they realized that the knots were five human beings clutching fast to the rigging.

Nothing more could be seen of the ship itself save the end of the jib boom. Corbel estimated the wreck to be scarcely half a mile off shore. Waves crashed heavily upon the beach and the sea raged and foamed as far out as they could see.

Corbel wondered how long the small human knots in the rigging could endure hanging there, ravaged by wind and rain and cold. Could he and his crew possibly reach them in time? While he was thinking, out on the vessel one of the men lost his hold on the ropes, fell into the water below, and was gone. The keeper cursed. There was little hope of rowing out to the vessel in such heavy seas. He decided to try firing a line aboard.

Selecting a point where, if he allowed sufficiently for the wind, the line might reach the ship, Corbel took careful aim and fired the Lyle gun. With tremendous force its projectile soared into the air high above the waves. The crewmen held their breath, sure it would reach, but the line began to curve downward in the air and the projectile plummeted into the sea after traveling barely more than half the distance.

The crew shot repeatedly but each time the projectile felt short. It would be a miracle if they could rescue any of the shipwrecked men, Corbel was beginning to feel. During the afternoon neither wind nor sea abated. First dusk threw a blanket of darkness over the scene that made further efforts impossible.

The keeper of Wash Woods and his crewmen started out before dawn the next day, and, as they watched, the rigging slowly separated itself from the gray downpour. Four figures still clung to the mast ropes, the driving rain pounding their bodies. One man had managed to wrap himself in a tattered sail affording some protection against weather.

Members of the lifesaving crew stood around chilled and frustrated as they stared out at the men in the rigging. They prepared their boat for launch. For a few minutes the downpour seemed to lessen slightly, and Corbel shouted, "Launch her!" Surfman Bonney, his face ashen with fear, refused to pick up his oar.

"Launch her!" Corbel roared again, this time glaring at Bonney, who still didn't move. The rest of the crew were in the boat and the keeper stared at Bonney with contempt. His refusal to go out with the men was an act of cowardice so unusual among the proud Outer Banks lifesavers as to be almost unknown. Malachi Corbel would fire him that night.

The crew pushed off but waves hammered the small craft, tossing it about wildly, then hurling it back on shore. They tried to row out to the shipwrecked vessel repeatedly, until they were exhausted, and each time they were fortunate to escape with their lives. It was the third day of rain and gale winds, and one by one crews from three other stations along the coast arrived to join the men from Wash Woods.

Keeper Corbel could not remember when a storm this intense had endured so long. His eyes strayed constantly to the rigging. The crews decided to send for a tugboat from Norfolk to rescue the survivors and they dispatched the message. Another seaman lost his hold on the ropes and was swallowed by the sea as Corbel watched.

Corbel strode up and down the beach, now pinning his hopes on the tug and clenching and unclenching his hands as he stared out at the mast. How long would the tug take to reach them after the message was received? He watched the three men left in the rigging, amazed that they had held on this long.

Malachi Corbel had no way of knowing what was happening to the north. The help the crews were waiting for would never arrive. Thwarted by the same raging seas, the tug was forced back to her berth at Norfolk.

As he waited, Keeper Corbel strode back and forth on the beach wearing his hip boots in the high water. Alternately, he prayed and cursed—praying to a God in which he had a certain primitive faith and cursing the relentless force he was battling. The wind seemed only to increase in fury. The duel between the keeper and the hurricane grew more desperate.

Would they reach the men in the rigging that afternoon before the curtain of rain and mist obliterated them from view forever, perhaps to be cast up weeks hence somewhere along the shore? Lord, what horrible sights he had seen on that beach. He had found the battered bodies of children, the remains of men and women partially devoured by sharks.

Like many an Outer Banker, Malachi Corbel was no stranger to death in all its forms, but now his thoughts turned to the tug which would come to their aid, and his spirits lifted.

His eyes searched out a big man still in the rigging whom he had watched defy death for almost two days. The figure was still there. What strength—what enormous will to live.

Corbel stood perhaps fifty yards apart from the other crewmen, his coat billowing about him in the gale. Up on the rigging, the fellow's head seemed to turn in his direction. Malachi Corbel was certain the man was staring at him, and he felt an overpowering sense of wordless communication. Lifesavers and victims were caught in an ordeal of fearsome days and nights, each striving superhumanly to defeat a brutal force.

The sea seethed and tossed relentlessly. It was impossible for Corbel to reach the wreck by boat even with his determined lifesaving crew. He set the men collecting driftwood, and when dusk came they lit fires along the beach, to cheer both the men in the rigging and themselves.

Wreck of a wooden sailing
vessel at dawn on Hatteras Island

Seaman Robert Lee Garnett had signed on the *Henry P. Simmons* in Philadelphia but that day was beginning to blur in his mind. Cold and wet, he had managed to wrap himself in a sail but his body ached from the long hours in one position. Only with the greatest caution could Garnett move his hands and feet, and from time to time, he was able to capture a little rainwater in the sail. He drank it greedily.

He watched one of the men on the beach walk back and forth and sometimes gesture as if directing other men. In the midst of his ordeal this man caught his attention and, somehow, gave him hope. More and more often he found himself dozing. He increased his efforts to stay aware of the feel of the rough rope in his stiff and bloodied hands. He must maintain his grip. Night came and he tried not to think of the tossing black water beneath him. The crews waiting for help received word that the tug could not leave Norfolk.

When Keeper Corbel arrived on the morning of the twenty-sixth he dreaded looking out at the rigging, but miraculously the big man and two others were still there. Three times he commanded the lifesaving crews to launch a boat. Each time the immense watery arms of the sea seized the small craft and hurled it back on the beach.

As the lifesavers watched helplessly, one man toppled from the rigging into the sea only to be followed without a cry by another. Two men erased from life as soundlessly as the stroke of a sponge wipes clean a blackboard.

Corbel and his crew set out in the surfboat to rescue them. The men rowed desperately. Their arms hurt as if the force of the waves would tear them off.

For a moment the crew seemed to be making headway. Then, as if the sea had merely been teasing them, leading them on, an oar snapped and a monstrous wave tossed the boat on shore. Malachi's breath came in aching gasps and his hands were a mass of broken, bloody blisters.

He was overwhelmed with hatred for his wild and wicked adversary. Here, on this string of off-shore islands, the sea birthed men like him. It fed them, was a beloved mistress and a respected taskmaster but also a monstrous tyrant. If they did not suffer death from its violent hands, at the very least they could be left broken and maimed for life.

Now, only one of the shipwrecked five still lived. Robert Garnett clung to his perch, his arms numbed. Salt spray ripped into the tortured, tender skin on his face. He cursed but endured, scarcely aware of being more than a numb appendage of the mast—a pair of eyes stinging from wind and water and a tired, tenacious brain. He had borne three nights and three days in this vicious storm.

Until the outline of the masts was lost in the mist and darkness, Malachi watched the lone figure. He was gripped by anxiety that this man might lose his ability to hang there, that he might slide, then plummet into the cruel water below. Driftwood fires sprang up along the shore and burned brightly. Perhaps they would cheer the fellow in the rigging, if he was still there to be cheered.

On the morning of the twenty-seventh, Corbel was back at Pebble Shoals before dawn. The weather that day was no more favorable, the rain falling heavily, but the man was still there. Toward evening the storm had nearly spent itself, and there was the promise of a shift of the wind to the westward. This encouraged Corbel. If the sole survivor could only hold on one more night, he would be saved.

By midnight the wind had become a moderate breeze, and before daylight the surfboat edged into the water. Strapping on their life belts, a crew of handpicked men, with Keeper O'Neal of False Cape and Corbel himself at the steering oar, rowed out to the ship. Malachi Corbel called out in the darkness and to his relief a faint reply came. Corbel called back encouragement.

When it was daylight they saw him, still wrapped in the sail. Robert Lee Garnett began to climb down stiffly and painfully. He had survived four days in the wind and storm.

Corbel and his men carried him to the station.

That night Malachi eased his weary body into the chair at his desk. The ordeal, begun four days ago, was finally over. Seaman Garnett, fed and now asleep, lay in a bed nearby.

Elation overwhelmed Corbel. He had wrested the life of one man from his old and ruthless adversary, the sea. But the keeper was tired and he wrote in his journal briefly.

> *One shipwrecked seaman waiting at the station to recover his strength. Feet both swollen badly from exposure.*
>
> *Malachi Corbel*
> *Keeper*

❖   *The details of this true story are in the annals of the United States Coast Guard along with the entries made in his log each day of the storm by Keeper Malachi Corbel.*

The Lovely Apparition

Beautiful Lydia haunts the highway
pleading for help, and no mortal man can help her . . .
though many have tried

There are few men who do not hold within them some experience which time cannot erase. For some men that experience is a woman. And for Burke Hardison it will always be Lydia.

Nor is he the only man who has encountered her. Since 1923 this young lady has appeared from time to time at her favorite spot. Men who have tried to help her have all told the same story afterwards. The story has been one of complete bewilderment and mystery.

Burke Hardison met Lydia late one rainy night in the early spring of 1924. He was on his way back from Raleigh to his home in High Point. The evening had been spent with friends made during his college years at State. And it must have been almost two o'clock as he neared the little community of Jamestown.

All around him the countryside slumbered under a billowing blanket of fog. Even the most obvious landmarks had silently vanished and there was an air of unreality about the misty world through which he drove. Along with this air of unreality came the feeling that all other life had ceased to exist save himself.

For miles there had been no other cars, but his eyes still strained as he peered through the mist for tail lights ahead. In front of him loomed the Highway 70 underpass. For a moment the fog seemed to clear. He was no longer alone. At the mouth of the underpass stood the slight, graceful figure of a girl. Dressed in a white evening gown, she flung her arm upward signaling desperately for him to stop.

Even before he pulled to the side of the road, he knew she must be in some terrible distress. He opened the door of the car as she came toward him.

"Please, will you help me get to High Point?" pleaded a soft, tear-laden voice.

"I'm on my way there now, and I'll be glad to help you," replied Burke. A gust of fog entered the car as the girl slid in beside him. He could see the pale blur of a lovely face surrounded by a halo of dark hair. And the diaphanous cloud of her white dress rested on the seat.

After she had given him the address of a street he was vaguely familiar with, they drove in silence. Nearing High Point he felt that he must find out more about her and began to question her.

Her name was Lydia and if there was more than that it faded into the fog. Her words seemed almost detached and so faint that he could hear them above the sound of the motor only with the greatest effort.

She seemed deeply distressed at the late hour and afraid her mother would be worried about her. Gradually he gathered that she had been to a dance that evening in Raleigh. But what had happened and how she came to be standing alone in the fog at the underpass, she either could not or would not tell him.

At times she failed to answer him at all.

"Why do you question me?" she finally asked. "Nothing is important now but that I'm going home."

So nothing more was said. He found the street she had given him and there stood the house on the corner just as she had described it. Well, he would not bother her further.

Opening his door, he got out and walked around to the other side of the car. Then he held the door open for his young passenger. But as he stared into the blackness of the car's interior he gasped in amazement.

The car was empty—his companion gone. Nor was there a sign of any living being near it. The only movement was that of the fog as it swirled in front of his headlights. For a moment he stood as if dazed, with his hand still on the door. Then such a cold chill swept over him that he slammed the car door and pulled his coat close around him.

Perhaps she had slipped into the house without his seeing her. He knew that he must find out. It was several minutes before his knock was answered and then it was not Lydia who opened the door. But the resemblance was there in the face of the old lady who confronted him.

"I'm Burke Hardison and I just brought your daughter home but she seems to have disappeared. Is she here?" asked Burke.

For a moment the old lady didn't answer. He could see the bright shimmer of tears welling into her eyes behind her glasses and she seemed to crumple before him.

"Are you trying to play some cruel joke on me?" she said. His bafflement turned to anger and he would have answered harshly but the tragedy in her face was genuine.

He explained how the young girl had stopped him at the underpass and begged him to take her home. And then he told how he had arrived at this address only to open the door of the car and find that she had disappeared.

"I had an only daughter named Lydia," said the old lady. "A year ago she was killed in a wreck near the underpass as she was coming home from a dance." Tears slid helplessly down her cheeks.

"This is not the first time people have tried to bring her home. But somehow she never quite gets here."

❖ *And the reports continue year after year from people who see her and attempt to deliver her to a house in High Point!*

Run
of the Ghost Train

*Mrs. Lowry was a little girl when
she stepped from the track to let the southbound train
go by. She never forgot what happened then.*

There is little in the realm of the supernatural which can quite match the fascination of a ghost train. It holds a unique grip on the human imagination.

An eerie headlight flashing down the track followed by empty, rattling coaches. The wail in the night of a lonely, haunting whistle as it echoes over quiet countryside.

North Carolina ghost lore would not be complete without the story of just such a train.

In the fall of 1906 the tiny lumbering town of Warsaw contained only a few country stores, a small family-style hotel, and numerous sawmills.

A short distance from town beside the tracks of the Atlantic Coast Line railroad lived the family of Henry McCauley. Each night when Mrs. McCauley finished her work at the hotel her family would meet her and together they would walk home down the railroad tracks.

It was late one November night and the fields around Warsaw lay white with frost. The McCauleys walked along the trestle leading toward their home, talking occasionally in low tones. The only other sound was the crunch of their footsteps on the stones between the ties.

Suddenly the sharp whistle of an approaching train pierced the cold autumn air. "Hurry, we're going to have to run to get to our crossing," shouted Henry McCauley to his wife and daughter.

The huge headlight was so close that it seemed the train was almost upon them. They ran panic-stricken across the trestle toward their crossing, gasping in the cold air until their chests hurt. Too winded to talk, they reached safety and stood waiting for the train to pass.

Up the track ahead shone the headlight just as bright as before. Again there was the sound of the whistle. They waited and wondered but no noisy, smoke-belching engine hurtled past them out of the darkness. In fact there was nothing—no real train at all.

It was the ghost train again.

The McCauleys weren't the only ones to see the ghost train. Several nights later the train from Norfolk to Wilmington approached Warsaw. The heart of the train's engineer leaped to his throat.

The single track ahead of him was brightly illuminated by the headlight of an approaching train. A train where no train should ever have been. He reached for his brake and there was the sound of wheels screeching in the night. Even before he had brought his train to a stop trainmen jumped off and started up the tracks to investigate.

But they soon returned shaking their heads and with nothing to report. As far as anyone could tell there was no train there! A puzzled engineer and his crew went on their way. From that night on they would slow as they reached the spot but they didn't stop again.

What was the reason for the ghost train?

The ghost train started making its eerie run after a tragic accident. "I was just a little girl when it happened," recalled Henry McCauley's daughter, who later became Mrs. Kirk Lowry of York, South Carolina. "It gave me a queer feeling—one that I never want to have again."

Mrs. Lowry's story began on a crisp November morning of 1906.

"I was walking down the track on the way to my grandmother's one morning when I heard the whistle of the southbound train. The old people called it the 'Shoo Fly.' Why, I don't know, but they always had and I guess they always would.

"I stepped off the track to let the Shoo Fly go by, and I'll never forget what happened then."

At one moment the train was chugging down the track toward the child who stood watching. The next moment there was a horrible wrenching sound and the monstrous black engine twisted to one side as if in agony. Then, still emitting huge puffs of steam, it careened wildly off the track and turned completely over. Behind it the baggage car gave a mighty lurch and came to a halt leaning crazily at a forty-five degree angle.

"The first thing I remember after that was a man's voice screaming for help from the baggage car."

By now passengers were piling out of the Pullman and men were trying to dig their way through tons of baggage to reach the buried baggage master. He died of a broken back before they could get to him.

In the cab of the engine all was quiet.

The engineer and fireman never answered the shouts of those who sought to rescue them. They had both been scalded to death.

The accident was the strangest kind of freak. The night before the ill-fated Shoo Fly went chugging along on its Norfolk to Wilmington run, a northbound freight stopped at the siding.

There was a saw mill next to the track and the freight train picked up one timber-laden car after another. Then the freight train had been moved out of the siding.

As the last flat car went by the main line track switch, a protruding piece of timber hit the switch and opened it. Three men were to die as a result.

By the next morning when the southbound Shoo Fly was due, the open switch had still not been discovered. Disaster was inevitable when the train hit the open switch at full speed.

Gilbert Horne, the engineer killed on the Shoo Fly, had been in railroading since he was a boy. How natural that his son Will should follow in his father's footsteps.

But what a tragic coincidence that the son should be engineer of the freight which had reopened the switch and caused the death of his father!

The little girl who ran with her parents along the railroad trestle never forgot the wreck or the ghost train which followed it.

"I saw that light with my own eyes and heard the whistle," she said thoughtfully. "Where the ghost train came from or where it went to, I never knew. But it went by our house almost every night 'til we moved away."

The Mysterious Hoofprints at Bath

For more than 175 years the mysterious hoofprints have been a reminder of the harsh bargain young Jesse Elliot struck with the devil

There've been lots of tales about the hoofprints, but it was just a simple thing. Like the marks where an automobile accident was. Old Ed Cutlar looked off his front porch toward the woods as he talked. The land he saw had been owned by the family for generations.

"Folks used to leave their horses loose down there in the woods on Goose Creek. Some fellows from Bath, 'specially one called Jesse Elliot, used to do a lot of racing on Sundays.

"This Elliot, from what I always heard, must have been a pretty high livin', reckless sort. On this particular Sunday a crowd of them was down at the creek readyin' their horses and talking about what each could do.

"Elliot jumped on his horse and started down the racing lane gallopin' like fury." Mr. Cutlar paused, and then went on: "'Take me in a winner or take me to hell,' he shouted to his horse.

"He'd no more than said it 'til the animal leaped in the air, dug her hoofs in the dirt and threw him slam against the side of a big pine."

Jesse Elliot was killed on October 13, 1813. The story as Ed Cutlar told it had been handed down in his family for almost one hundred and fifty years.

"When I was a child we'd pull up grass and take bark and put it in the prints on our way home from school. Next mornin' they'd be just as clean as can be.

"One time my Uncle carried corn out there. He called his hogs and threw the corn all around and in the tracks. You know they wouldn't touch the corn that fell in those hoof-marks?" He stopped and pondered a moment.

"I say his death was a warnin' to people not to make such heavy impressions" was his final word on the subject.

The farm house where Ed Cutlar lived, one mile west of Bath, is two hundred and fifty yards from the hoofprints. One can still see the strange looking hollow places in the ground. The holes are about the size of saucers. And they are bare of grass or any kind of growth. A short distance from these depressions in the earth is the rotted stump of an old pine tree. It is said that hairs from young Elliot's head clung to the pine bark for months. Finally that side of the tree died leaving the other side still green and living.

Nothing covers the hoofprints for long, although many skeptics, including a newsreel cameraman named Earl Harrell, have placed debris over them. The next morning he, like countless others, returned to find the marks clean and no trace of the debris in the impressions.

A descendant of Jesse Elliot confirms the date of 1813 as that of his death. But according to the story of an old family slave it was not Sunday but Christmas Eve. In this version, an annual race was to be held January 6 and he was giving his mare a workout when he was killed.

Several years ago a man leased the area from Cutler and set up a soft-drink stand there. He roped off the place containing the hoofprints and charged admission to tourists.

Wild young Jesse Elliott may not have made a harsh bargain with the devil. Ed Cutler and the natives of Beaufort County believe that he did. If he didn't, how else would you explain the mysterious hoofprints?

The Fairy Cross

*He felt the pressure of the fairy cross
in his hand and knew that he would believe
the legend forever*

Season follows season in the mountains of Western North Carolina and some of the more isolated areas seem to have been little changed by the passage of time. Red and gold maples are gradually disrobed by winter winds and the black tracery of their limbs makes outlines against the pale winter's sky. Days turn into weeks until once again spring surges through the valleys and slopes leaving tender green leaves and wild flowers in her wake.

There is something in this process which heals broken hearts and so it might one day for John Sebastian and his daughter, Selina. It had now been almost a year since he began his duties as a hired hand for the old couple on their small farm in the North Carolina mountains.

The Sebastians were different from the mountain people and the old man and his wife had been quick to sense it. Although nearly a year had now passed since the arrival of the Sebastians, the couple had never penetrated the father and daughter's reserve.

Tonight, grateful for the warmth of the fire on the crisp fall night, the four were clustered around the hearth.

The inroads which sorrow had made on the face of the father did not escape the old man. Nor did the look of pain in Sebastian's eyes when he saw the old man tenderly place a cushion at his wife's back.

As it began to grow late and only the flickering fire light pushed the darkness back, the faces became a blur to each other. Somehow this made it easier to speak of that which was nearest the heart. The increased intimacy encouraged the old couple to probe in a kindly manner and finally the tide of emotion John Sebastian had long held back overflowed and he found release and comfort in words.

Almost ten years ago he and his wife Anna with their infant son and six-year-old daughter had saved enough to go back to Anna's homeland and visit her parents.

It was a joyful reunion for all. The old people saw and adored their grandchildren. He and his wife again attended the village church where they had first met during the gaiety of a religious holiday.

All too soon it was time for them to leave. In the early morning hours of the day of departure, he and his six-year-old daughter were roughly awakened and seized by the secret police. His own questions and his wife's pleading and tears had no effect, nor were they given any assurance of when they would see each other again. "In a few hours the future lay bleak and shattered around us," said Sebastian.

"All that was left to me was Selina," and he reached toward her, covering her hand with his. "We were put on a train and sent out of the country with warnings not to try to take Anna and my little son back to America."

"In the long years since, I have entreated the authorities of the country to allow them to come to America. Many kind people have tried to help us, but no one has yet succeeded."

When he was finished there was a long quiet broken only by the crackling of the fire. The old couple said little, knowing through experience the time when words bring slight comfort.

Finally, the old man began to reminisce about the days of his youth and from his experiences during years of real poverty, threaded with humor and love, he went on to talk of the mountains themselves and of the legends surrounding them.

"Have you ever heard of the fairy crosses?" he asked.

"No," said Sebastian. "Would you have me believe in fairies?"

"You must judge that for yourself," replied the old man. "I only know that I have seen fairy crosses with my own eyes although they are very difficult to come upon.

"Years ago when these mountains were young, all of the caves and the hollow trees along with the sheltered places in the woods were inhabited by a fairy people. They were a happy, carefree lot laboring little and much given to frolics.

"One night in early spring they were dancing merrily around a mountain pool. The pool is said to be not far from this cabin although I myself have never been able to find it.

"While they were dancing a messenger arrived from the spirit world to tell them that the Son of God had been crucified on a cross. As they listened tears began to fall from their eyes. Each tear falling to the ground formed a tiny but perfect cross.

"On rare occasions one of these crosses is found by men. Among the Cherokee Indians they were believed to possess strange and wondrous powers."

Pulling himself up from the chair with the stiffness of age, the old man said goodnight to Sebastian and his daughter. Sebastian decided to fold several blankets in a sort of pallet and lie down to look into the fire. There was a self-forgetful fascination in staring at the flames and soon he found himself dozing off. Several hours later Sebastian awakened and his thoughts turned to the alternating despair and hope with which he had lived for so long. He got up and opened the door of the cabin.

The faint flush of dawn was just beginning to appear along the tops of the mountains. He decided to go out and walk for a while alone. His daughter and the old man and his wife were sleeping soundly.

Lost in his thoughts he took first one trail and then another. With each turn he continued to climb upward until he found himself on a steep, rocky path leading into a little clearing. Here he decided to rest. Leaning back against a rock, he gazed out across ridge after ridge of purplish blue mountains, their peaks just emerging from diaphanous layers of clouds. It was a breathtakingly beautiful sight. But his climb had thoroughly exhausted him and he fell asleep.

Once again, he heard the clear, sweet tones of bells. He was with his wife, Anna. It was a bright, sunlit day and they were on their way to the small village church to celebrate the holiday. He saw her face—the dark hair growing back so smoothly from the temples and the deep-set smoky blue eyes—as she walked beside him. His little boy's fingers were clasped tightly around his own.

After a time, John Sebastian became aware of the rocky, uneven ground beneath his body. He opened his eyes on the brilliant October morning and at first thought he must have awakened in the palace of some Midas of old. The glowing colors of the fall foliage surrounded him. A small animal scurried through the underbrush near him and for the first time he was conscious of the rocky ground and the cramped position of the arm on which he had rested his head.

He realized his hand was clenched tightly around a tiny object. Relaxing his fingers he looked curiously at the little brown piece of stone in his grasp.

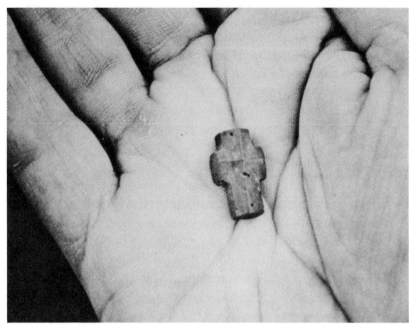

To his surprise he found that it was a tiny but perfect cross. He had never seen anything like it before. Certainly, he had not had it when he had fallen asleep heartsick and exhausted. He recalled the story the old man had told him—the story of the fairy crosses and their miraculous powers. This diminutive but perfectly formed cross could only be one of the fairy crosses. Sebastian looked at it long and wonderingly.

Still holding it tightly in his hand he began to descend the path and find his way back toward the cabin where he knew his daughter must long have been awake and wondering at his absence.

It was not until he was perhaps halfway down the mountain that he became gloriously aware of something. There was a difference in the very heart of his being. The weight within him which he had carried up the mountain during those early dawn hours was miraculously gone. In place of the pain which had wrapped itself tightly about his heart for so long, there was a sense of joy and peace.

Nearing the end of the trail which led to the cabin, he saw his daughter running toward him. Tears streamed down her face and for a moment it seemed that his heart would stop beating. But as she reached him he saw that they were tears of happiness.

"Mother and Jan are coming to us—at last! The news came just a few minutes ago. They will finally allow them to leave."

John Sebastian held his daughter close and said nothing. For what did he need to say and what did he need to know? He felt the pressure of the fairy cross in his hand and he knew that he would believe the legend forever. Believe that somehow his own tears and those of the fairies had been seen and blessed by the One for whom the fairies' tears were shed.

Music
by the Ghost Organ

To this day no one can explain
why the organ played at old Kadesh Church

A carpenter of sorts, Horatio Carter was a rolling stone. He would not have had it any other way. He liked to meander from town to town, stopping for a few months wherever the mood struck him.

Since late summer he had been making his home in the small community of Kadesh in the rolling green hills of upper Cleveland country.

On this particular October afternoon shortly after the close of World War I, he could have been seen walking up the hill from which Kadesh Methodist Church surveyed the surrounding farms. A battered straw hat shielded Horatio from the hot autumn sun and under his arm was a satchel containing his carpentry tools.

As he walked he hummed a snatch of the "Muskrat Ramble" and with more humor than sorrow meditated on the quirks of a fate which had kept him poor.

Entering the front door of the old church he found the window with the rotted sill and set about his task of replacing it. He had been at work for possibly half an hour when he heard footsteps at the rear of the church.

There was the sound of a chair scraping on the wood floor. And then the bellows of the organ emitted an introductory wheeze. In a few seconds the church was filled with music. But it was music the like of which Horatio had never heard before. It was neither hymn nor ballad. Nor did it resemble the minstrel tunes of which Horatio was so fond.

It was like the soft rustle of the night wind through the trees or the melodious pleading of a harp plucked gently by unseen fingers.

Leaving his work, the carpenter walked down the aisle toward the organ. There was an eerie quality about the perfectly blended chords of the unknown melody. As he approached they died softly away, the last notes lingering for a moment in the air about him.

What Horatio saw when he reached the organ was startling indeed. The chair at the organ was empty, the choir loft deserted. With a terrified cry the itinerant carpenter fled, his work forgotten and his tools unclaimed.

Early the following afternoon the minister of Kadesh Church knocked at the door of the farmhouse where Horatio boarded. Much to his surprise he found that the carpenter had left that morning.

"That poor fellow was took near crazy," said the good woman who answered the preacher's knock. "All he could say over and over was he wouldn't work no place where organs just went to playing themselves."

The puzzled minister shook his head in bewilderment. He confided the incident to several of his church officers but they were as much at a loss as he.

"Might be he was helping hisself to some white lightnin' while he wuz workin', preacher," offered one of them, smiling broadly.

It was a night in late November and the biting cold of winter had wrapped its frost-white cloak over the fields of the little foothills community. A prominent Kadesh farmer rode hastily to fetch the doctor for his wife in labor. As he approached the church he could have sworn he heard strains of music wafted toward him by the wind. Slowing almost to a stop, he listened.

An unearthly melody was coming clearly from the direction of old Kadesh Church. On and on played the weird music emanating from the pitch dark church silhouetted against the moonlit sky. But the frightened farmer had no desire to linger and hear it out.

Word of the mysterious music at Kadesh Church began to spread. Others claimed to have heard it but none stayed to investigate.

One Sunday night services were brought to a halt by the start of a dust storm. After the congregation had gone, the minister finished closing the windows to shut out the fine cloud of dust which was blowing in and beginning to settle everywhere.

Finally, he was ready to leave, but on this night the heart of the Kadesh pastor was heavy. Only a minister comes to know the deep frustrations, guilt, and heartbreak of the people he serves. Oftentimes the load can be overwhelming and so it was for the pastor tonight. He decided to sit down alone and read a few passages from his Bible.

So absorbed was he that only gradually did he notice that his thoughts were accompanied by the softest of melodies. Familiar with church music as he was, he could not recall ever having heard anything similar. It floated about him with a strangely haunting quality.

He walked toward the organ feeling that he must see this organist who could play melodies of pervasive sadness with such consummate skill. As he approached, the music grew very soft, then ceased altogether. When he reached the organ he froze with disbelief. For where he had firmly expected to see some unknown musician, he found himself confronted only by an empty chair.

Nor was there anyone to be found in the choir loft. Its door was bolted just as he had left it. The minister edged forward for a closer look at the organ itself. Over its stained oak top lay a coating of dust. He drew an exploratory finger across the keys. They too were coated with the fine grey film.

And now as he stared at the coating of dust on the keyboard the minister was certain of one thing. No human hands had been responsible for the music in Kadesh Church.

Bummer's End

*Fifty corpses swung from the trees in the swamp . . .
and another dangled over two new graves
in a quiet family cemetery*

Near Smithfield in Johnson County is a swamp. A short distance from its shore—almost hidden by mist—lies an island. The sunlight is shut out by trees and matted vines. It is a perfect setting for a ghost.

But no fictional, storybook ghost lurks among the cypress. Instead, the swamp is haunted by the ghosts of fifty real men—men who died the way they lived.

It was the twilight of the War Between the States. In North Carolina Sherman had cut a devastating path across the state. In his wake came the dregs of war—the bummers.

They were men who belonged to no army, stragglers and riffraff who plundered and took what they pleased because there was no law, no order, no force left to stop them.

The swamp today is much the same as it was that night during the 1860s. A night when scores of trees bore a gruesome burden. Altogether there were almost fifty bodies swaying in the breeze when morning came.

The story of the swamp and that night of vengeance starts at a plantation home near Smithfield.

Colonel John Saunders had returned to his home to recover from a Yankee bayonet thrust in his hip. Late one summer night he and his wife awoke to the sound of a loud banging on the front door.

Saunders painfully made his way toward it. His wife lay in bed listening to the soft dragging sound of her husband's useless leg as he went to the door.

"Who's there?" he called out.

"David Fanning, sir," came the reply. "I have a sick man and am badly in need of shelter for him."

"What division?" asked the Colonel.

"Wheeler's Confederate cavalry," was the answer.

Saunders opened the door and as he did so rough hands grabbed him. Pain shot through his hip like liquid fire. Surrounding him in the yard were two dozen hard-faced ragged men on mules.

The man who seemed to be their spokesman was somewhat better dressed than the rest. He wore two revolvers and a cavalry sword swung at his side.

"All we want's a little information," said he.

"Bummers, eh," replied the Colonel contemptuously. "You'll get nothing from me."

"Oh, won't we, old fellow?," said the leader impudently. "Show us where you keep your money and jewelry."

Colonel Saunders refused.

"String him up, men! Bring out his wife and hang them both from the same tree."

And the bummer struck Saunders brutally across the face.

By daybreak all that remained of the Saunders home was a huge area of still smouldering timber. Nearby a single pig which had escaped the plunderers rooted in the ashes.

Several weeks later a young officer stood before his commander, General Joseph Wheeler.

"Sir, I would ask permission to hunt down the bummers who murdered my parents," said Saunders, his eyes dark with pain.

"I cannot direct you on a mission of personal revenge," replied Wheeler, "but this I will do. Take twenty men into Johnson County and do everything possible to rout bummers wherever you find them. They are important sources of supplies to Union troops in this section. You have my permission to go after them."

Day and night young Saunders and his men sought out bummers, shooting and hanging them as they went. But there was no sign of the group they hoped to find.

They were ready to return when word came that the Rance Massengill plantation had been burned to the ground. Bummers were reportedly camped near the end of Devil's Race Track eight miles below Smithfield.

The bummers must have sensed danger for by the time Saunders and his men arrived they had fled toward Hannah's Creek Swamp.

Excited country people ran from their homes to stop Saunders and his men as they passed. "They're in the swamp. There's an island in the middle with fifty men on it," went the talk.

After some thought, Saunders decided he would lose too many men if he attempted to rush the island. "Go home and come back with all the old clothes you can find," he told the country people.

A few hours later it was dark. Dressed in the old clothes, Saunders and his men set out in boats for the island. The light of their torches cast fiery, dancing images on the black swamp water.

A challenge rang out from the island.

"Who goes there?"

And the men in the boats replied, "Bummers from Harnett County. To hell with the Confederacy!"

They were welcomed with glad shouts. Leaving their rifles stacked in their camp the bummers rushed to the boats to greet their comrades.

Too late they realized that these were no friends. Twenty armed men eyed them with cold relentlessness.

"Who is your leader?" asked Saunders.

"David Fanning, at your service," answered a bold voice and a tall bummer stepped forward.

"My name is John Saunders. Is it familiar?"

Fanning's swaggering manner dropped from him and his face grayed. "Why it must be . . ."

"Yes, I am Colonel Saunders' son," said the young Lieutenant quietly.

"Search each man," ordered Saunders. Forcing the reluctant Fanning to lift his arms, Saunders searched his pockets. Beneath his handkerchief in the pocket of his coat he felt a small object cold to the touch.

As he drew it out a fine gold chain fell to the ground and in his hand lay a gold crucifix—his own mother's.

"Hang every man of them, but not Fanning," ordered Saunders.

The two waited together as one man after another was strung up. When there were none left and the dark figures of the bummers hung silently in the moonlight Saunders mounted his horse.

With Fanning cowering beside him, they rode to his father's plantation. Past the blackened ruins toward the family cemetery they rode. Two new headstones shone whitely under the limbs of a tall tree.

Placing a noose over one of the branches, Saunders drove Fanning's horse from under him. For almost an hour Fanning hung there holding the rope with both hands. Finally the hands loosened and slipped from the rope.

For years afterward natives said that on moonlight nights shadowy figures could be seen hanging from the trees near the swamp. And few there were who cared to go by it after the sun had set.

Only the chimney was left standing when Sherman's bummers burned the Saunders plantation.

The
Little Red Man

The cellar of the Brothers House
at Old Salem was once haunted by a playful ghost

It was March 25th of the year 1786. Just thirteen years earlier the first Moravians had settled in Salem.

Single Brother Andreas Kremser, stood looking with quiet pleasure across the sunken garden behind the Brothers House. For some years now he had lived here with the other unmarried men of the religious community.

Like his companions, he prayed, he sang, he cooked, worked at his trade of shoemaker, and occasionally gardened. Andreas looked at the lovely shades of the flowers made more brilliant by the glow of twilight.

His thoughts went back to his boyhood in Pennsylvania. The long-forgotten odor of spring lilacs was strong about him. He remembered his bitter longing for the parents he had never known. At the age of three he had been placed in a home and school for little boys.

Andreas was just sixteen when he had left Pennsylvania to carve out his future as a shoemaker in North Carolina. For brief intervals he had done kitchen work and even swept chimneys. But chimney sweeping was not for him and he recalled that task with irritation.

How ridiculous to criticize his chimney sweeping just because there had been an epidemic of measles. Yet that is just what had happened. But he had told them—the mayor, the civic leaders, and anybody else who criticized his chimney sweeping. The chimneys were miserably constructed and there were too many for any one man to sweep.

His thoughts returned abruptly to the present and he realized it was almost dark. He must get ready to attend evening services.

That night after worship he felt wakeful and restless. There was excavating in progress in the cavernous "deep cellar" of the house where an addition was planned. Perhaps he should work for a while before retiring. It was only about eleven.

The cellar's depths were cold and damp. There were no windows and the brothers worked by the light of the flickering candles. Taking up a shovel he joined the others. They cast long, eerie shadows as they worked to hollow out a place under the clay bank.

It was easier to work on his knees. Andreas scarcely heard the warnings of those watching that the bank was almost ready to go. Suddenly there was a shout: "Jump back. It's breaking off!" The men threw themselves backward, but Andreas still on his knees could not rise in time.

It seemed as if tons of the damp, smothering earth descended on him. With frantic efforts his fellow workers managed to dig him out. His left leg crumpled beneath him and his whole body felt numb with pain.

Brother Lewis who was a doctor gently removed Andreas' red jacket. He opened a vein in the wounded man's left arm but little blood would flow. At about two o'clock the blessing of the Church was bestowed upon him. Shortly afterward the spirit of Andreas Kremser left his body.

From that day on the brothers would often times hear a sound like the tap-tap-tap of a shoemaker's hammer. Each would glance quickly over his shoulder but never saw the shoemaker at work. Occasionally as they walked through the shadowy basement passageways, the last of a red coat would flit around the curve just ahead. "There goes Kremser," one brother would whisper to another.

Finally there became less and less need for a home for unmarried brothers. The last of the brothers moved out and for a while families made their home there.

A few years later the Church used the house for widows of the congregation. Halls which once rang with the songs of the young men now listened to the muted voices of elderly ladies reminiscing of their youth.

A child visiting her grandmother ran to tell her, "Betsy saw a little man out there and he did this." The little girl crooked her finger to show how a hand had beckoned to her.

Some of the old ladies told of glimpsing a little man with a friendly smile. But their stories were shrugged off with amusement.

Then one day a prominent man of the community was showing a friend through the old cellar. As they went he related the story of the "Little Red Man." Both were highly amused. It was not until they turned to leave that all at once—out of nowhere—there he stood.

With arms outspread the two men tried to corner him. They closed in only to grasp empty air. Eluding them, he reappeared at the end of the gloomy chamber and grinned merrily.

Several years later a visiting minister ended the career of the "Little Red Man" forever. An invocation to the Trinity and the words "Little Red Man go to rest" exorcised the friendly chap who hasn't been seen since.

The
Thing at the Bridge

Aaron Lee was a scholar. He couldn't explain the
unearthly horror at the bridge . . . until Old Squire died.

T ime is such a relative thing that to an insect a few
days may be a lifetime and last month eons away. To the
thoughtful among us, it is but a slight strain to break the
bonds of time and imagine that a hot, still day in May of 1820
is our own today.

It is easy to feel the heat of that sun beating down
upon our face and shoulders. And shading our eyes we see
again the white man and the black man hoeing cotton
together along the bank of Mill Creek in Johnston County
near Smithfield.

They are master and slave. To look into the heavily
lined face of Lynch is to see a face at once both ignorant and
cruel. The slave, "Old Squire," has the red hair characteristic
of Lynch's field hands. The unusual hue was said to be caused
by their diet. Lynch fed them on Hayman potatoes and cow
tallow.

Today the black man's labors seemed only to anger his
master. When he slowed for a moment's rest the lash fell
across his back with a crackle. If a sprig of grass remained in
the row behind his hoe, the whip curled swiftly through the

air again, stinging and burning like a streak of liquid fire on the sweaty, shining black flesh.

The two men continued to chop closer and closer to the bridge across Mill Creek. For a moment Squire looked up welcoming the approach of dusk. Lynch caught him at it, cursed, and once again lashed out with the whip. Squire turned and the full, searing impact struck square across his face.

But this time the whip had met and ignited kindred violence. Almost of its own volition it seemed that the shining blade of the slave's hoe made a swift arc in the sunlight—an arc which ended with crushing impact on the forehead of Lynch. Without a sound he fell to the ground. For a few seconds Squire stood over him, horrified at what he had done, still holding fast to the blood-covered hoe.

Then seizing Lynch by the feet he dragged him under the bridge. He hollowed out a grave quickly in the damp earth, working with fearful urgency lest he should hear the sound of footsteps approaching the bridge. When he finished his grisly task he crawled cautiously from under the bridge and in a moment had faded into the dusk around him.

On the following day Lynch's absence was noted by his slaves, and local whites supervised a search party. The search was a fruitless one, however. And no further efforts were made as Lynch was regarded with as little esteem by his white neighbors as by his own slaves.

Among these neighbors was a highly educated gentleman named Aaron Lee who lived on top of the hill overlooking Mill Creek. An eccentric bachelor, he devoted himself to books and breeding fine horses.

As was only natural when stories began to circulate of weird events at the bridge, the opinion of such a scholar as Aaron Lee was sought. Local folk told of the sound of trace chains rattling under the bridge at night, of torches ceasing to burn when the bearer set foot upon the bridge and mysteriously starting to blaze once more when he had crossed. On one occasion a heavy cane left a man's hand to be thrust back into it again as he reached the other side.

Finally the curiosity of the man of letters needed to be satisfied. On a late autumn afternoon he took one of his best mares and rode down the hill toward the bridge. His crossing was uneventful, and, enjoying the fine weather, he continued on for some distance.

It was nightfall when he reined his mount about-face and began the homeward journey. All went well until he reached the top of the long sloping hill down which flowed Mill Creek.

At that moment a cold gust of air seemed to rise from the waters of the creek and envelop both horse and rider. Simultaneously Lee felt something land on the horse behind him and cling with a heavy pressure against his back, a pressure so chilling that icy waves penetrated his very marrow.

Instantly the gait of his mare broke from a spirited canter into the slow dragging walk of a plow horse. She moved with great difficulty as if weighted down with a load almost beyond her strength. Lee's first impulse was to leap off his mount and flee from the frigid thing pressing close to his back. With a strong effort of will he held to his self-control.

At length the human rider, the horse, and its ghastly burden reached the bridge. As the mare's hoofs touched it, the terror-stricken Lee heard the most agonizing groans coming from beneath the timbers of the bridge.

It was the pain-wracked voice of a man engaged in a death struggle. And although most of the words were indistinct, one was plain. That was the word "Squire."

As the horse cleared the bridge the frightful cries stopped. But the icy rider clung close to the shrinking horseman. And the horse itself seemed near the point of exhaustion as she ascended the hill near Lee's home. As they gained its crest there was a convulsive movement from behind Aaron Lee and the thing accompanying him was gone as quickly as it had come.

Relieved of her strange burden the terrified horse leaped forward and galloped with such frantic speed that Lee had ridden two miles past his home before he was able to rein her about. When they reached home the mare was wet with foam and sweat. Her wind was broken and never again was she her former high-spirited self.

It was not long afterwards that the time drew near for Old Squire to die. In the closeness of the tiny slave cabin he fought his writhing conscience at every turn. Finally he sent a pathetic plea to the scholar on the hill, begging to see him before he died.

Aaron Lee came and he listened as the old man poured out his gruesome and somehow pitiable story. There was no need for Lee to question it. The meaning of the word which he had heard coming from under the bridge now fell into place.

Seeing that Old Squire had just a few hours to live he tried to reassure him as best he could. Lee left the slave's cabin shortly after nightfall, knowing the slave would never live to be brought to trial.

It was early the next morning when Lee decided to exercise one of his horses. He started down the hill toward the bridge and was but a few feet away when he saw upon it the outstretched body of a man. Riding up to it he was amazed to recognize the lifeless figure of Old Squire.

He would have sworn that the old man could not have risen from his bed, so weak was he the evening before. How had he come to arrive at this spot fully a mile from his cabin? It was a mystery Aaron Lee was never able to explain satisfactorily to himself. He became more and more withdrawn and pensive.

But he told and retold the story of his fearful ride and the end of Old Squire. In the years that followed it has been a common sight at night to see a light bobbing up an down around the bridge. And those who saw it would say, "See, there is Lynch lashing Old Squire now to his heart's content."

Devil's Tramping Ground

No one questioned his Infernal Majesty's right to this piece of ground

In this age of science there are fewer and fewer mysteries of nature that remain to challenge man. Does the Devil have favorite haunts on earth? Does he pay nocturnal visits to these spots?

Yes, say the natives who live near the "Devil's Tramping Ground" ten miles west of Siler City.

Just off a country road near Harper Cross Roads is a perfect circle in the midst of the woods. It is forty feet in diameter. Surrounded by pines, scrub oaks, and underbrush, the circle itself is bare except for a type of wire grass.

The narrow path around the edge of the circle brooks no growth of any kind. Sticks or other obstructions put in the path are never there in the morning.

According to Chatham County natives, it is the Devil whose nightly presence discourages the growth of anything fresh and green and good. Round and round the well-worn path he paces, concocting his evil snares for mankind.

Who can tell? To the best knowledge of those living nearby, no one has yet dared to spend the night at the "Devil's Tramping Ground" and spy on his Infernal Majesty.

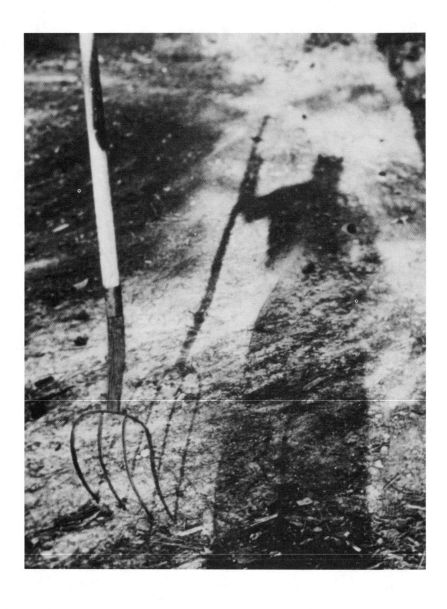

The Reverend Edgar Teague, a retired minister living
a short distance down the road, tells of a group of young men
from Bennett who dared one of their number to spend the
night there. He took the dare, but Mr. Teague says that along
about 11:30, as he was driving home from his brother's house,
he passed a blanketed figure heading toward town as fast as
his legs could carry him.

Efforts have been made to explain the circle. The most
popular theory holds that it was an Indian meeting ground
where roaming tribes gathered periodically for feasts and
celebrations. These always included the vigorous, aban-
doned dancing of the braves.

The rhythmic movements of countless moccasined
feet accompanied by drums throbbing through warm summer nights could well have made a bare spot. But the feet and
their owners have long since been gathered to the Great
Spirit while the surrounding underbrush still grows to the
edge of the circle and stops.

Less glamorous is the theory that the circle was made
by the hoofs of horses circling around and around to power a
mill for grinding cane. This would be more feasible if there
were not other similar spots now well overgrown.

Several scientifically minded investigators have noted
the presence of salt nearby and concluded that the soil here
has too high a sodium chloride content to encourage plant
growth. This theory, however, cannot explain the perfection
of the circle or the narrow path encircling its perimeter.

One of the most startling discoveries came when soil
tests were made by the North Carolina State Department of
Agriculture. Results showed the soil within the circle to be
completely sterile.

This only serves to compound the mystery. Soil is
known to replace itself. Why should this soil just within the

bounds of the circle remain sterile from the time of the earliest settlers while just outside of it plant life abounds?

It will take further word from science to disprove Satan and among the natives it is still the gentleman with the pitchfork who casts the larger shadow at the "Devil's Tramping Ground."

To this day no plant or tree will grow on the spot the devil treads.

The Light at Maco Station

*Over the years this flickering light
has eluded all attempts at explanation*

There was fog in the low places and out of the blackness overhead fell a fine, steady rain. It made little ponds of the ruts in the lonely country road.

Hugged by scrub pines, vines, and underbrush, the road straggled for perhaps a hundred yards. Then the woods stopped abruptly and there lay the wet, softly gleaming rails at Maco Station.

Maco lies fourteen miles west of Wilmington on the Wilmington-Florence-Augusta line of what is now the Atlantic Coast Line Railroad. It is today much as it must have looked to Joe Baldwin years ago.

Joe was conductor of a train headed toward Wilmington that rainy spring night of 1867. Just fourteen miles from home his thoughts turned to his family. Would his wife be up to greet him?

Even his train sounded as if it were glad to be on the home stretch. There was something comforting about the chugging noise of its wood-burning engine. For the moment Joe forgot the shower of soot and sparks which he battled daily to keep his coaches clean.

It was time now to go through the cars ahead and call out the station. He glanced proudly at his gold railroad man's watch. The hands of the watch read three minutes 'til midnight. Just about on time.

He tugged at the door at the end of the car. The night was so dark he couldn't see the outline of the car ahead. As he managed to open the door, he swung his lantern a little ahead of his body. The foot outstretched to step forward stopped in midair. There was no car ahead! He was in the last coach of the train and it had come uncoupled.

Panic surged through him and for a moment he could hardly get his breath. His first thought was of the train which followed his own. He must signal them. They had to know there was a wild car in front of them.

He raced back through the car. With one mighty heave he wrenched open the heavy door at the rear and was out on the platform. He felt his own coach losing speed and as it did he saw the huge, fiery eye of the train which followed him.

He began to swing his lantern back and forth, back and forth, more furiously as the distance between him and the advancing train grew smaller.

The pursuing train plunged on through the night, its cyclops eye burning balefully. With terrific impact it hurtled into the rear of the runaway coach completely demolishing it. In the collision Joe's head was severed from his body.

A witness said that his lantern waved desperately until the last, then rose in the air, and inscribing a wide arc, landed in a nearby swamp. It flickered there for a moment and then the flame continued burning clear and strong.

Not long afterward lovers strolling near the railroad late at night reported seeing a strange light along the tracks.

It would start about a mile from Maco Station—just a flicker over the left rail. Then it would advance, growing brighter as it came up the track. Faster and faster it seemed to come, swinging from side to side. There would be a pause and it would start backwards, for a moment hanging suspended where it had first appeared, and then it would be gone.

Watchers over the years have said that the light is Joe Baldwin's lantern and that Joe is hunting for his head. Once the light was gone for over a month but it always comes back. Joe seems to prefer dark, rainy nights.

After roads were built in the area, skeptics maintained that the light was merely a reflection. Several years ago all traffic in the area was blocked off while a group of observers watched for the light. Joe appeared, swinging his lantern as usual.

A short time before, a company of Fort Bragg soldiers armed with rifles decided to put an end to Joe's nightly excursions. His lantern eluded both guns and soldiers.

Over the years railroad engineers have sometimes mistaken Joe's light for a "real" signal. As a result the railroad ordered its signalmen at Maco to use two lanterns, one red and one green.

The tracks have been removed but strangely enough the light continues to return, and those who have seen it say that the ghost of Joe Baldwin still haunts Maco looking for his head.

Dromgoole

Peter Dromgoole had disappeared
as completely as if he had been spirited away

At the western edge of Chapel Hill is a high wooded cliff. The view from it is beautiful, and the spot is frequented by young lovers. Why does it seem to attract tragedy?

In recent years two young men have committed suicide nearby. Not far from the cliff lies a rock with mysterious stains which resemble blood. Is this rock the only remaining clue to the untimely death of an earlier university student?

In 1833 a youth named Peter Dromgoole arrived from Virginia to study at the University. He had been there only a few months when he met and fell deeply in love with a beautiful Chapel Hill girl.

There are few campuses which equal the loveliness of the University of North Carolina in the spring. It must have been particularly appreciated by young Peter Dromgoole that spring of 1833.

He and Fanny had their own secret meeting place—a huge flat rock near the cliff. Some afternoons when Fanny arrived before Peter she would sit on the rock watching the sunlight drift through the leaves above.

It was never long, however, before she would see Peter's tall figure striding toward her along the winding road which led to the rock. One balmy spring day followed another so happily that these two could hardly have sensed the approaching tragedy.

Then Peter noticed that another student—a close friend of his—was also interested in Fanny. Gradually Peter's jealousy grew until finally it became an unreasoning thing which knew no bounds.

He made every effort to avoid his former friend but the other youth seemed to delight in goading him. One afternoon the two met face to face on one of the narrow dirt walks of the campus.

His rival's shoulder hit Peter's with such force as they passed that Peter's hat was knocked to the ground. The rage which had been smouldering within Peter rose and enveloped him. His face flushed and heated words flew between the two young men.

The other youth challenged Peter to a duel. The challenge was no sooner flung down than it was accepted.

Each chose his seconds. The spot agreed upon for the duel was to be near the cliff at the edge of the town. The hour was set for midnight and plans were laid with the utmost secrecy.

Peter was a reasonably good shot but the night of the duel was such that marksmanship good or bad scarcely mattered.

A warm May evening, it had rained briefly and a low lying mist clung to the ground wrapping itself tenaciously around students and trees alike. The two young men and their seconds made their way carefully toward the cliff.

Before they realized it the protagonists were almost upon each other. As they backed off for the agreed upon ten paces their figures assumed an almost ghostlike quality. Two shots rang out and the seconds rushed toward the young man who lay on the ground.

Blood covered the front of the ruffled white shirt. Even as his second attempted to lift his head Peter Dromgoole gasped and breathed his last.

Terrified, his rival and the two seconds dragged the lifeless Peter away from the cliff and toward a huge rock. Digging frantically—lifting their heads at each strange sound from the woods—they finally managed to dig a grave deep enough. They lifted Peter's body from the rock, placed it in its shallow grave, and replaced the earth as carefully as the darkness and their haste would allow.

Meanwhile Peter's family had received a strange letter from him. A letter which warned that he might bring sadness upon them and that they would probably never hear from him again.

This was the last they ever heard from their son. A few weeks later his uncle, at the insistence of Peter's mother, made a trip to Chapel Hill. In the room which Peter had shared with a young man named John Williams were the only signs which remained of him—his trunk and a few clothes.

Peter Dromgoole had disappeared as completely as if he had been spirited away. His fellow students were unable to give any clues as to what had happened to him. Stage coaches leaving Chapel Hill showed no record of any passenger named Peter Dromgoole.

His uncle returned to Virginia a saddened and extremely worried man. His trip had been fruitless and with not one clue to his nephew's whereabouts.

This version of Peter's death and disappearance was related by a former student as he lay on his deathbed some sixty years later. It may or may not be the true story of the strange fate of Peter Dromgoole.

But what of a Chapel Hill girl named Fanny?

For many a long summer afternoon she waited at the rock for her lover. What strange brownish stains had suddenly appeared on it! Sometimes as the shadows lengthened she would think she saw a tall figure striding toward her

The bloodstained rock lies in the shadow of Dromgoole Castle.

through the woods. Then she would put her head on her arms across the rock and sob quietly. Her agonizing questions were never to receive an answer.

According to another story young Peter ran away from school and enlisted in the army. However, the muster rolls of his supposed battalion have never been found.

Is the name of Peter Dromgoole upon them? If so, the yellowed pages lying in some forgotten cache hold fast to their secret.

Ghost
of the Old Mine

Gold Hill was once a flourishing boom town. And the tiny,
peaceful community still remembers its violent past.

Twilight is the hour to see a town if you would sense
its true spirit. When evening falls in the tiny community of
Gold Hill near Concord the present fades and shadows of the
past begin to live again.

The superstructures of old gold mine shafts jut darkly
grotesque against the sky. An immense deserted mine office
building crouches brooding beside the country road.

At the village crossroads is a general store reminis-
cent of the early 1900s. Everything about this out-of-the-way
place echoes the past. It is a shell of a once vibrant community
with its heart gutted out. The stuff that once made the blood
course lustily through the veins of this town was gold.

Suppose by some accident of time we should arrive in
Gold Hill during the days when it teemed with life. How
excitingly different the town looks to our eyes! It is rowdy and
bustling with the smell of smoke in the cold December air.
Heavily bundled figures jostle each other along the muddy
main street.

Occasional boisterous peals of laughter come from The Nugget saloon and the murmur of soft Latin voices mingles with thick Cornish brogues. Gold Hill is booming in this year of 1842. It is bursting its shoddy seams with Jew and Gentile, Latin and Nordic, Cornishmen and Negro slaves.

Rough, uneducated men are converging on it from every direction, drawn by their lust for gold. Among them Aaron Klein was a misfit. Son of a rabbi—almost too gentle for his own good—what did this young man have to do with the greed and anticipation swirling about him?

Aaron himself couldn't have explained it. His parents had died several years earlier, back in Pennsylvania. Just twenty, this not quite boy, not yet man, had landed in Gold Hill.

It was a week before Christmas and Aaron leaned against one of the store fronts watching a motley group stumble out of The Nugget. They might have passed him unnoticed if it had not been for the sharp eyes of "Big Stan" Cukla. His tremendous physique made the nickname well earned. And no amount of whiskey seemed able to dull his amazing bodily coordination.

For reasons of his own he had taken an intense dislike to Aaron. Some smiled slyly and said it was rivalry for the heart of a lovely blue-eyed Cornish girl named Elizabeth Moyle.

Big Stan stopped abruptly when he saw Aaron standing in the shadows.

"Have a drink little Jew boy," he called out tauntingly. Aaron made no reply. The big man's face reddened, the muscles of his short neck bulged, and the ugly little eyes, too small for the coarse features, glared in hatred.

One huge arm shot out and grasped the back of Aaron's neck.

"We'll see whether you're too blasted good to drink with me," he roared. Holding a bottle in his free hand he tried to force the fiery liquid between Aaron's lips.

The youth coughed, spluttered, and finally managed to free himself from the grip of his tormentor. He half stumbled, half ran toward the doorway of a store behind him.

"She doesn't want a sniveling, sick puppy. She wants a man!" were the last words Aaron heard as he reached the shop's door safely.

But Big Stan Cukla was wrong. He often bragged that he knew the shafts of the mine as well as he knew his own little shack, but he did not know women.

It could not have been more than a week later when word that Aaron and Elizabeth would marry on Christmas Eve spread among the log cabins, shacks, and covered wagons of Gold Hill.

Every hour that Aaron labored in the depths of the Randolph mine he hated it more. But the odious work brought him nearer the day when he and his bride could go North and begin a new life together.

As Christmas approached, young Aaron's happiness knew no bounds. Even the days in the mine's dark tunnels seemed to fly. Before, he would think of the black nothingness of the 850-foot shaft below as the skip would lower him down to his level. Now, he hardly thought of the water and darkness in the depths beneath his feet.

The miners and their wives enjoyed joshing Aaron about his coming marriage. But there was one whom these crude but good natured jokes only made more taciturn.

Big Stan's hatred of Aaron had become a seething, burgeoning thing within him. Sometimes at the sight of

Aaron it would rise in his throat as if it must find release or choke him.

A few nights before the wedding Aaron returned to his tiny shack to find that a puppy he had been caring for was gone. Calling and searching through the broomstraw back of the row of shacks he heard a whimpering sound. It came from the direction of the Randolph shaft. The whimpering ceased as he drew closer.

At the entrance to the shadowy shaft he found the still warm body of the puppy—its head crushed by a heavy blow.

And then there must have been another sound, perhaps a half-mad roar of animal-like satisfaction. On Aaron's part there could only have been a terrible surge of panic at the brute strength of his antagonist before oblivion came.

The following morning when the first of the miners arrived at the shaft they found the body of a small dog nearby. One of them dug a shallow grave for it with his pick. Accompanied by raucous laughter from his comrades, he leaned on the pick handle, head bowed ostentatiously, and held a mock funeral service.

Aaron Klein did not appear for work that day and by the morrow the whole mining village knew he had disappeared as completely as if he had been translated.

Elizabeth Moyle's eyes were like dark, sad windows where someone was dying inside. Big Stan came to her father and suggested leading a search party through the countryside around Gold Hill.

"Just so youse ud be knowin' if the boy been done harm," said he.

The searchers returned cold and exhausted after walking for miles through the woods and fields and discovering not a sign of Aaron Klein.

Several months later people began seeing a ball of light near the mine shaft at night. The light would travel toward the row of shacks. Women fetching water at dusk would come in breathless saying the light had followed them. Some would say it was accompanied by a sound like a puppy whimpering.

An occasional miner returning home late at night from the Gold Nugget would swear that the light had been close on his heels every step of the way.

As the days went by money continued to be plunked with careless exuberance on the counters of the business establishments in Gold Hill. Most of these immigrants considered themselves wealthy beyond their wildest dreams.

All but Stan Cukla. When his pudgy fingers touched the gold, he touched it as if he were caressing a woman. For Big Stan had deluded himself that this yellow dust could buy him the favor of the blond Elizabeth.

Even before he had sent his rival plunging to his death in the depths of the mine shaft, the big man had worked secretly in the tunnels at night. The light from the candle on his cap would move methodically along the tunnel wall. It was a tiny flame which floated and bobbled in the sea of surrounding blackness.

Almost a year had passed since Aaron's death when one night long after midnight, Stan Cukla was digging the precious ore. It might have been his aloneness, for sometimes the light of his own candle seemed to him to be reflected back from the darkness around him. Every so often Big Stan thought that about halfway up the tunnel he could see a light flicker. It was a light about the size of his own which moved along at the same pace he did. Only lately the light was nearer.

On this December night he was sure that he saw it again—closer still. He tried to concentrate on his work but his breath began to come faster. Soon his heart began to pound so frantically in the stillness that he could hear its beating. The light's glow appeared to travel faster along the wall.

Its tiny circle of brightness was now visible out of the corner of Big Stan's eye. Then it was at his side. He could have died rooted to the spot, but he had to turn and see it.

Before his eyes stood a dripping, faceless thing. On its cap sputtered a candle.

With a horrified cry, Cukla lunged past the figure and fled toward the skip which would lift him to safety. The light followed close behind, seeming to gain every time Cukla's heavy boots would slip on the loose shale floor of the tunnel.

Big Stan's hand finally brushed the beams which frame the mouth of the tunnel and he stepped out of it toward the skip.

But the skip was gone.

Where it should have been there was nothing but black emptiness. And the heavy, terrified body of Big Stan plummeted down—down—down.

The following morning the miners coming to work were surprised to find that the skip was not at the ground level. Pulling it up by the cables they found the body of Stan Cukla. And judging from its appearance he must have fallen many, many feet before he struck the floor of the lift.

There was much speculation as to how he had met his fate. But all any of the men actually knew was that he must have entered the mine the night before and after he had gotten off at his level the skip had somehow continued to go down until it had reached the bottom of the 850-foot shaft.

Stories about the mysterious light which seemed to come from the direction of the Randolph shaft continued to circulate for a number of years. Shortly after the Civil War it was seen no more. But the remains of the superstructure of the old Randolph mine continued to loom tall and sinister.

The Battle of the Dead

In 1905 two hunters witnessed a
Civil War battle fought forty years earlier

One of the most fascinating possibilities which grips the human mind is the reoccurrence of scenes from the past. There have been stories of midnight rides, romantic trysts and duels re-enacted. Those who claim to have seen these things can describe the appearance and action of the participants with amazing detail.

Most of the attempts to explain these strange phenomena have been based on the theory of exact duplication of atmospheric conditions. This freak of nature may occur so rarely as to be glimpsed by few mortals. But none has yet ventured to say whether these stories are in the realm of the scientific or supernatural.

Jim Weaver who lived near Smithfield in the early 1900s, never forgot the terrifying events of the night he visited the past. Weaver made no effort to explain it. He simply knew that it had happened. He was there, he saw it, and he told the story for the rest of his life.

A man of medium height and somewhat slight build, Jim Weaver was a farmer and a miller. Smithfield folk called him the "Blue Man." He was subject to a mild form of epilepsy and the nitrate of silver remedy of those days turned its users a bluish color.

Although he worked long and hard, Weaver and his family seemed always in the throes of poverty. He was a quiet, serious fellow and his only boast was that he had never told a lie.

Jim's weakness was his love for hunting. Many a night he and his dog went after the wary possum in the woods of Bentonville near his home.

Late one Saturday night in March, he and an Englishman named Joe Lewis were walking along through pine trees and thickets. When the staccato barks of Weaver's hound rent the night air, the two men knew the dog had treed a possum.

Jim Weaver had always felt a man ought not to hunt on Sunday. He glanced now at the moon sinking lower and lower in the sky. He was aware that it was probably already midnight. But there was surely a possum in that tree and he had to get it.

In order to do so he decided to chop down the small tree where the hound had stationed himself. Grasping his ax he drew back and struck a resounding blow. As he did so there came a blinding flash of light from the top of the pine. Badly startled, Jim let his ax drop from his hand and stood paralyzed with fear while one flash after another erupted in the surrounding trees.

They illuminated the woods about him. And he could see shadowy, uniformed figures running to and fro, dodging behind trees and stumps. Each carried an old-fashioned rifle.

All at once from behind Weaver came the rush of horses. Gray-clad riders—a ghost cavalry—thundered past. There was the hum of bullets and the crackle of musketry. Men in blue uniforms were running, shouting, shooting from behind the trees and dying in horribly grotesque positions.

From nearby rifle pits heavy shot tore through the branches of the trees and ricocheted from their trunks with a vicious snap. Still the two men stood rooted to the spot. Their knees felt weak and their foreheads were beaded with cold perspiration. The woods all around them were full of the sound and fury of battle. Bullets hissed past them like hail and peppered trees and soldiers alike.

Then about ten yards away from them, Jim saw a desperate encounter take place. A Yankee soldier was attempting to wrest the flag of an advancing Confederate unit from its flag bearer. A second gray-clad figure came up to help defend the standard. The Yankee turned and with a lunge pierced him through with his bayonet.

Now the Yankee and the young Confederate soldier with the flag under his arm struggled together. Finally, hatless, his face streaked with the enemy's blood, the flag bearer suffered a knife thrust to his shoulder and fell to the ground.

Only a few minutes had probably elapsed before Jim Weaver and Joe Lewis began to run. Fear spurred them on while their hearts thudded wildly and their throats ached. They passed the old Harper House in their flight. But they did not pause to watch the balls of fire illuminating the dark sky behind it nor to marvel at the strange light streaming from the windows.

On they fled until in utter exhaustion they threw themselves flat on the ground near the kitchen house back of Weaver's log cabin.

The Harper House where lights were seen
was used as a hospital during the war by both armies

On the night that Jim Weaver and Joe Lewis hunted
among the old trenches and earthworks of Bentonville,
almost forty years had passed since the Blue and Gray had

fought and died there. It was on this very ground that Joe Johnston sought to prevent Sherman's sixty thousand men from joining with Grant. The battle began on Sunday, March 19, 1865. It continued through Tuesday the 21st with artillery fire crackling far into the night.

The nearby Harper House was used as a hospital for the wounded and their screams had shattered and shocked and entreated for several days.

Jim Weaver long ago joined Smithfield's Confederate veterans to whom he told his story of the night he saw the battle of Bentonville with his own eyes. Believe him or not as you will.

But there was one among those veterans who knew Jim did not lie. Only seventeen years old on that night in 1865, he had served as flag bearer for his unit. His left arm still hung useless at his side from the shoulder wound he had received while trying to retain his unit's flag. His older brother had died in an effort to help him.

The
Ghost on the Stairs

The beautiful old house has seen many sights since it was built in 1800 . . . but none so strange as the lovely lady in black

It was a few years after the turn of the century. And a gay party of Fayetteville girls with their suitors surrounded the piano in the parlor of the A. S. Slocumb home.

Lovely young faces reflected the flattering light of kerosene lamps. Strains of a popular romantic ballad drifted through the halls of the antebellum mansion.

A young lawyer leaned against the parlor's magnificently carved marble mantel. His intellectual face was pensive. Absentmindedly his finger stroked a small nick at the mantel's corner—supposedly the result of a shot fired by General Sherman.

At the moment, however, the barrister's mind was neither on Sherman nor on pretty girls. He was absorbed by an agonizing mental struggle. Was he really happy in his chosen field? Or were his years in law school meant to be forever wasted?

Perhaps the way to resolve the warring forces within him was to be alone with his thoughts. Almost oblivious to the merrymakers, he crossed the parlor and walked toward the wide archway opening into the hall.

And then he stopped dead still, his heart caught in his throat. Something or someone was floating toward him down the stairs. It appeared to be a diaphanous feminine figure. Before reaching the foot of the stairs she hesitated a moment, then turned almost sadly and started back toward the landing.

There was the flutter of filmy black and all at once she disappeared as if rounding an invisible corner.

Overcome with amazement the young man went out into the cool spring night. In the past he had listened with amused skepticism to the strange stores told of the old house.

Built in 1800, the house was used for a short while during the 1820s as a United States bank. There were rumors during the Civil War that the old bank vault was the entrance to an underground passageway to the Cape Fear River.

A man had supposedly been murdered there before the War Between the States and his body hidden in the basement bank vault. Some said that his fiancée, dressed in mourning, went up and down the long stairway searching for her sweetheart.

Many years have passed since our friend saw the apparition on the stairs. Later the house resounded with the happy footsteps of young career women. Living in this beautiful old home run by the Women's Club, they took little thought for the ghosts of yesteryear.

Occasionally they paused to admire the handsome oil painting done by the famous artist Elliot Dangerfield. His father owned the house during the 1860s. They enjoyed showing visitors the impressive ballroom built by another owner, John Sanford, for his wedding.

But the walls know countless secrets. They have heard many sounds. The echo of General LaFayette's boots, the tinkle of gold coins in the bank vault, the hushed voices of Confederate soldiers, the boisterous shouts of occupying Yankee troops, the dull thud of carpetbags dropped in the hall.

The marble mantel in the parlor still has the soft sheen imparted by the hands of Italian workmen long years ago. How much have its skillfully carved figures seen?

Without a doubt they know of the lady in black and her story.

And what of the young man who saw her? He gave up his plans for a law career and entered the ministry.